The Puritan Jungle

AMERICA'S SEXUAL UNDERGROUND

BOOKS BY SARA HARRIS

Nonfiction

FATHER DIVINE: Holy Husband

SKID ROW U.S.A.

CAST THE FIRST STONE (with John M. Murtagh)

WHO LIVE IN SHADOW (with John M. Murtagh)

NOBODY CRIES FOR ME

HOUSE OF THE TEN THOUSAND PLEASURES

HELLHOLE

LORDS OF HELL (with Lucy Freeman)

THE PURITAN JUNGLE: America's Sexual Underground

Fiction

THE WAYWARD ONES

The Puritan Jungle

AMERICA'S SEXUAL UNDERGROUND

by Sara Harris

G. P. Putnam's Sons   New York

Contents

Introduction

THIS is a report on the shocking but inevitable results of our national ethic—the Puritan attitudes that have guided our thoughts and actions since our nation's inception. No two worlds, on the face of it, could be farther apart than that of the upright, moral Puritan and the seething underworld inhabited by America's sexual outcasts. Yet the two are intertwined, interdependent. They feed upon each other, nurture each other, and indeed cannot exist without each other. The search in Puritan America to satisfy one's sexual impulses and patterns, even to provide simple gratification, has driven many people underground —into a savage, terrifying jungle. I decided to write this book because I was aware, though not deeply as I am now, of the tragedy of such people. I didn't know them as people when I first contemplated this book, of course; nor, to my knowledge, did many others. Fiction writers have portrayed the sexual underground and its inhabitants poignantly, movingly; but figments of writers' imagination cannot possibly sound sufficiently authoritative to en-

7

able most of us to identify with these people or comprehend their world. As for nonfiction interpretations, these have been, if anything, less satisfying—unfeeling and impersonal statistics of a world that, though so separate and distinct it might as well be on Mars, lies only around the corner. I knew that world existed—we all know it exists—but like most of us I had never been exposed to its full impact or known the full depth of its tragedy.

I know now, and this book is a report on what I found in over two years of travel in towns and cities throughout America, in the Yokohamas, the darkest corners of New York, Washington, D.C., Philadelphia, Baltimore, Chicago, Peoria, Kansas City, Dubuque, Palm Beach, Miami, New Orleans, Richmond, Norfolk, Los Angeles and Hollywood, San Diego and adjoining Tijuana and Reno. I interviewed homosexuals—from male prostitutes and kept boys to homosexual "married" couples infinitely respectable in their public and private lives; lesbians; sadists and masochists; transvestites and wife-swappers; pill-takers, heroin addicts and votaries of LSD; blue-movie producers, the sad former beauty queens with lapsed Hollywood contracts who act in their more or less insipid offerings, and those involved in the filming of a terrifying pornographic movie in San Francisco's Tenderloin: a noted pornographer-photographer; the actresses—prostitutes and drug addicts; the actors, equally addicted; and a star known, for reasons that became all too frighteningly obvious, as the Gorilla, whose sadism the customers relish over and above the true-to-life pornography. I spoke at great length to many hundreds of people, and came to understand what it means to be a person cut adrift from society in an underground world. In a sense, I also lived in that world. I ate in their homes, met their friends and the few relatives with whom they still maintained contact, was made to feel welcome in their bars and other hang-outs, was a firsthand observer of their lives. No attempt has been made on my part to judge. The world they in-habit is, for most of us, even those of us who are trained observers, too alien for that. I felt it important that they reveal themselves, and therefore I relied heavily on the use of tape-recorded autobiographies. The participants—and throughout this book I have tried to go only to those directly involved—tell their own stories, in their own words, drawing their own conclusions.

I never paid anyone for a story. Never having been ap-proached by a "square" before, people seemed to need to clarify themselves and the reasons they had become what they had. Once they came to believe I was there to dis-cover and learn about them—not judge them, they had a great impulse to tell their story of life in an outlaw world "like it is," pulling no punches. They told about the trivia of their lives, the daily strains and stresses. They talked frankly. Their self-revelations were often extraordinary. Of course, they did not present the whole picture of them-selves, their lives, and their world. People don't. Members of an alien society, like people anywhere, pass over crucial areas because they are as familiar to them as the air they breathe. But so do generals talking about warfare. Or housewives talking about their homes and household problems. They explained elements of their personalities

I had never comprehended before; for instance, what lies back of their violent condemnation of some act bound to seem commonplace to the rest of us and their easy acceptance of one that would seem outrageous. In the intimate picture they gave not only of how they live but also of how they regulate their lives among the majority, they taught me always to be conscious of the eyes through which they look; their tricks of perspective, their special view of life.

If lesbians, homosexuals, hustlers, dancers in "topless" bars, sadists and masochists, and wife-swappers wear lenses unique to them, so too do those who uphold the Puritan standards and thus keep the jungles aroar—from the good middle-class mothers who are honestly convinced that if only they can shut evil out of their children's lives all will be well, to the pious pillars of society whose bias and loud animus keep pornographers and mail-order solicitors in business.

I interviewed dedicated homosexual-baiters, some of whom would be surprised to realize they were latent homosexuals themselves. I spoke to vice cops and leading citizens hot on the trail of wife-swappers (including one not above propositioning this writer to serve as his "wife" —for research purposes only!). The censors on Maryland's film censorship board—the only state movie censor board in America today—spoke openly with no fear of my tape recorder, styling themselves "liberal" God-fearing citizens who "hate filth" (and, in barely descending order, the Supreme Court whose recent rulings hamper their fight against filth). Their qualifications for ruling on what films

Marylanders of any and all persuasions should see: "I think being a mother's enough."

The Puritan Jungle is a report from these vastly opposed and generally little-known communities in America. No attempt has been made—except in the overall sense—to artificially balance off points of view. Again, the people speak for themselves.

The problem of selectivity was with me always. I interviewed so many inhabitants of the underground it was impossible to include them all. Those present in the book represent but a distillation of all I saw or heard—for the roots of the underground run deep and into many strata of society. For example, although the specific findings are not contained in these pages, *The Puritan Jungle* reflects my investigations into contemporary divorce (as seen by lawyers, judges, and especially unhappily married people from New York to California and on the Donner Trail Ranch, the last of the elegant divorce ranches in Reno) and abortion. I spoke with sick and lost unwed mothers, their lovers, parents and ministers, some sympathetic, some overtly condemning, as well as those who make their livings from "caught" girls and women: abortionist doctors motivated by genuine concern to untrained midwives working out of morbid, disgustingly dirty homes. These, too, like the prostitutes and blue-movie actresses I met and who *are* described in the book, pay the price of living in the Puritan Jungle.

I began this book in August, 1965, when I attended a convention in San Francisco, sponsored jointly by the Mattachine Society, organized by homosexuals to give help and understanding to others of their kind, the Daughters of Bilitis, a lesbian group with similar purpose, and the exciting and effective National Committee on Religion and the Homophile. I am grateful to Harold Call of the San Francisco Mattachine Society, Dore Legg of the Los Angeles Mattachine Society, Richard Inman of the Miami Mattachine Society, Dr. Frank Kameny of the Washington, D.C., Mattachine Society, Phyllis Lyons of the San Francisco Daughters of Bilitis, the Reverends Cecil Williams and Ted McIlvenna of the National Committee on Religion and the Homophile, who helped introduce me to the sad world of the homosexual in America. With them and many of their colleagues, I attended meetings of homosexuals and met "mod" ministers who, along with their wives, are identified with their "gay" flock; went to homosexual bars, homosexual parties, including those given expressly to introduce me to the scene. I learned, at first hand, the fear known by these men and women from San Francisco's Tenderloin to New York's Greenwich Village, their exploitation, the way society penalizes them and the hypocrisy by which they are made outcasts and outlaws.

John Paul Marat and John Coleman, a law student at San Francisco College, introduced me to the San Francisco and Chicago and New York male hustling life. I also met, as was inevitable for anyone spending time in male hustlers' hangouts, female prostitutes and their madams, pornographers and their models, stripteasers and topless dancers, who like many in this book must remain pseudonymous for their own sakes.

Of course this book could never have been written without the advice and constant encouragement of many distinguished fighters against sexual hypocrisy: lawyers like Stanley Fleischman of Los Angeles; Morris Lowenthal of San Francisco; Jake Erlich of San Francisco; Elmer Gertz of Chicago; police community relations personnel, including the highly regarded Dan Andreotti, formerly San Francisco police community relations director; officers of local Right to Read Committees, especially those in Chicago, Newark, New Jersey, New York, Los Angeles and San Francisco; and personnel of the national and local offices of the American Civil Liberties Union.

This, then, is *The Puritan Jungle*. I have sought to anatomize with detailed specifics the double standard nobody will be surprised to learn permeates our society . . . one set of rules for the rich, another for the poor . . . the tendency of the police to ignore the raffish doings of the well-heeled conventioneer and his big-business sponsor and to crack down on the outcasts . . . the venal activities of vice-squad officials who often use their official position to gratify their personal lusts. . . .

If by presenting the lives of those who must perforce inhabit this jungle, I have been able to provide the reader with some insight, understanding—and tolerance—I will be proud to have written *The Puritan Jungle*.

SARA HARRIS

The Puritan Jungle

AMERICA'S SEXUAL UNDERGROUND

I

"Who Needs Expert Testimony? Being a Mother's Enough."

CRISSFIELD, Maryland, the "crab capital of America," is geared to crabbers and their families. It has a single movie house showing nothing but family type movies and one small restaurant on the docks. There are also a few small shops where the crabbers—living on the adjoining island of Tangier, which does not welcome "foreigners" (all who do not come from generations of Tangier fishing families)—dock their boats, sell their fish, and shop for groceries, clothes, and other necessities not available locally.

Crissfield is near civilization, though—only miles from Washington and Baltimore—and on weekends it becomes colorful; the islanders sit in the single restaurant with their girl friends or wives, drinking beer and eating the best crab cakes served anyplace in America.

Crissfield was the home of the Maryland movie censor board's chairman, the recently deceased Mr. Egbert Quinn. He was a small man over seventy who had lived in Crissfield all his life. He had married and brought up three children in this town of 4,500, "of which perhaps thirty-five percent are colored and work in the oyster-shucking houses, the canneries, on the farm—that kind of labor." Quinn, when interviewed, was lean and enthusiastic and had the high spirits of a much younger person. He was very proud of his job as chairman of the censor board—Maryland is the only state in the Union with such a board—and even prouder of having been editor of Crissfield's only newspaper, a weekly, and having been three-time mayor of his town.

"So, in other words, I guess you can say I'm not disliked around here, no indeedy." He grinned an elastic grin to show big, white false teeth.

He was eager to tell how he happened to become chairman of the censor board. "I was in the legislature for many years in Baltimore and I usually hung out, almost made my headquarters, in the office of the board head they had up there in the legislature. It was near my office, and having quite a good bit of time on my hands, I looked at many of the pictures that came in and talked with the people who were running the place. I had a pretty fair understanding of their problems and what they were up against in trying to keep movies decent in Maryland.

"So, in other words, it wasn't something that was entirely new to me when the governor let me have the chairmanship of this department. Actually, he appointed me to a different position—but when I found that this spot was going to be vacant, I asked him to swap the other fellow. I thought maybe something could be done to improve the department. And then, that Supreme Court."

In his gentle voice he said that "those old men in the Supreme Court are the ones responsible for all those dirty pictures we've got today. It's terrible. Any picture that's got a story and so-called social significance is supposed to get the seal, be approved, according to Mr. Justice Douglas and the rest of them. A movie can be reeking with sex and immorality, so long as it's got social significance, you've got to let it by because the Supreme Court ruled you do. And here's something else: my committee's job, even with the pictures that are so bad we've got a chance of getting rid of them, is a lot tougher today than it was—mmm, say three years ago. Up until then, if a fellow showed his film to the censor board— which he had to do—and we didn't like it, didn't give it the seal of approval, well then, he accepted our decision. Or if he didn't, well, it was up to him, up to the manager or theater owner, up to the fellow who showed the film to take the case to court. The Supreme Court turned the whole thing around though and it said it wasn't up to the producer or the movie-house manager to prove why we should not give their picture the seal. Now, we ourselves have to take the case to court if the board disapproves a certain film and won't issue a license.

"Now," he said with an indulgent smile, "since I'm chairman of the board, when they [the movie managers] bring it in and we take it to court, the lower court, you know, we always win. So it should rest there, right? We don't like it, the lower courts don't like it. So why not

let our decision stand? But, oh, no, the way the Supreme
Court's working it, the manager or owner or whoever
can appeal to the Court of Appeals. He can say, regardless of what the lower court says, we're all wrong and
quote the Supreme Court or anybody else they want.
Well, until about a few weeks or so ago, when a picture,
a terrible, vulgar picture came before us and we wouldn't
want to give it the seal and the lower court agreed how
right we were, darned if it wasn't appealed to the Court
of Appeals and won in that court. So that's what makes
us so mad, but I got a way of getting around that Supreme
Court anyway. Sometimes."

Mr. Quinn's eyes were steel-bright. "That picture—
well, they heard a case down there in the Court of
Appeals and they looked at certain films—one of them
by the way was so vulgar that we showed it to the Senate
Committee the other day, even to the Court of Appeals,
and it was so bad they held a hearing on it the same day.
For the first time in the history of the censor board, the
Appeals Court upheld the findings of the lower court and
of the censor board.

"It was just one of those obscene sex things. No plot.
No nothing. One of those nickelodeon type things. But,
all the same, it could be shown anywhere in the state if
we gave it a license. It could have been shown even here
in Crissfield and anywhere else they had machines to
show them."

In addition to its three governmental appointees the
Maryland movie censor board had, in Mr. Quinn's
words: "a pleasant, hard-working and thoroughly dedi-

cated staff. There's this man who's classified as an account-
ant and could be said to be in charge of the office and is
the last word for staff when it comes to ruling on pictures. He has a sharp mind. And there's another man
there in the office that is classified as a motion picture
machine operator but actually he has a variety of duties.
Helps in the office and he helps view the pictures and
does very little machine operating."

The movie machine operator's qualifications for de-
ciding questions of decency are, Mr. Quinn said firmly,
"proper. That man's been running that movie camera an
awful long time," he said. "We used to have a lady
who'd been with the censor board, I think, about eighteen
years. For six years she was a member of the board and
for the past twelve she's been the chief reviewer of the
films. She actually knows more about the films—knows
more about assessing films as to their potential value
one way or the other, more about the laws of the various
states—than any of the rest of us. But she left and went
to work in another department. I think—this is my own
thought—she thought the board might be going to fold
up. The legislature might put us out of business.

"Some people have been trying it every year, two or
three distributors in Baltimore City—producing companies. They would rather not have censorship from
the standpoint that it costs them some money—in other
words, they have to send their films in to be looked at and
they have to pay a fee for it. So this lady thought they
might win and I think that's why she left."

Mr. Quinn, however, did not agree with his most experienced staff censor about the fate of the board. And so far he's been proven right. Despite the best efforts not only of producers and exhibitors of disputable films but also of members of civil liberties organizations and the overt opposition of Governor Spiro T. Agnew—the board continues secure in the pledged support of the majority of the Maryland legislators.

"The legislature, you know," Mr. Quinn illuminated, "isn't about to abolish us because the American Civil Liberties Union or the two-bit producers and exhibitors tell them to do it. No indeedy. Now they might be inclined to do something if the *big people* made a fuss. But the big people, you know, they would really rather have censorship. At a hearing on the board we had the other day, there was this lawyer who represents several of the big companies and that was exactly his view. He wasn't down in Annapolis to oppose censorship in Maryland. Because with the large companies, it's different than the fly-by-nighters. Sure, you'll have pictures coming in with an off scene, a bad scene. But that'll only be one small part of the whole. And the big movie men are cooperative. Well, I'd say that in 90 percent of the cases or more, all you have to do is talk with those people and tell them that you don't think that particular scene should be in the picture. And they listen to you. They go along with you and cut it out. Of course, the ten percent of the big producers aren't like the ninety though. They're terrible. They're as bad, maybe worse in their way than the fly-by-nighters are in theirs."

Mr. Quinn's "bad" producers and exhibitors include

"any of them who had whatsoever to do with such Hollywood films as *Who's Afraid of Virginia Woolf?*, *A Walk on the Wild Side*, *Night of the Iguana*. Well, I was married for forty years before the Lord took my good wife away, and there was never anything in all that time like some of those awful scenes in the *Virginia Woolf* picture. And my friends never knew anything like that. Nor my sons.

"But you can't do anything about it. They just laugh in your face and come to court with their experts trooping after them. Psychiatrists, educators, art directors; you name the expert, they have him. And what can you do, how are you going to fight?

"It's not just Hollywood, the law's behind the foreigners too, Italians, Swedes, French. They have terrible stuff but no matter how you feel inside you have got to give them the seal because the experts say so. It's art because it's foreign and it has got 'social significance' for the same reason. So it's like fighting city hall to try bucking the experts.

"Naturally, up till recently the Maryland censor board never used expert witnesses ourselves because we felt the defense would troop more and better experts in the courts than we could get. Even if we would win in the lower courts, the Court of Appeals would turn us down. But here lately we did troop into court with our psychiatrist and educator and art director. Well, maybe we should have done that before because for the first time in the board's history we actually won a case in the Court of Appeals.

"Well, this producer had no expert witnesses to our three. His movie was called *La Paree,* I believe. It had no dialogue, no music, no story. There was nothing. And I can tell you it wasn't fit for kids, or adults either, but certainly not kids.

"We don't have any authority though to make distinctions between pictures fit for children and those for adults. And what good would it do if we had?" he asked. "It might be fine and dandy if movie owners were, well, honest—if you could depend on their words of honor. But you can't because they don't care.

"Most offenders could put out a sign reading 'For Adults Only' and then, if you told them, 'Cross your heart and hope to die if you ever betray your word of honor'—why they'd cross their hearts and hope to die and *still* betray their words of honor if they thought there was a dollar in it. Because they're not churchgoers—most of them don't even believe in God and have no conscience. So what can you do? You can't believe them, no matter what they say."

Mr. Quinn said his committee had been appointed for purely "political" reasons. "I vote the Democratic ticket and have always been a good party man. But, I'm a liberal on this question of censorship and everything else. I'm about as liberal as anybody that comes along. I told the people down there in Annapolis I'm not a witch-hunter—not a crusader. But I do believe in decency."

Smiling warmly, Mr. Quinn talked about the other members of his board:

"There are two women besides me on the committee.

One is named Mrs. Avara. She looks at more films than anybody else. She's a bail-bond lady. She writes bail bonds. She's a businesswoman. Now, she's a woman of not much education but she's a woman of a whole lot of common sense.

"And the other lady is Mrs. Schecter. Her husband is— I think he's an attorney or in the real estate business. They're a family of the upper echelon, you might say. She has had many advantages in education."

Mr. Quinn said that Mrs. Avara "may be the toughest member we've got when it comes to judging films. She's so conscientious, you know, that's why. But she is guided very largely, as all of us are, by the opinion of the attorney from the Attorney General's staff. And he comes in—we get him in to look at films we don't like and if he says we can't do anything with it, except license it, why, we license it most of the time.

"I did hold up one film though once, myself, last week. I came home here to Crissfield Thursday and the attorney to our board went down Friday to look at it. And they called me about it because I said 'no seal,' but the attorney said there couldn't be anything done to keep it out because of the Supreme Court. I said, 'How long can you hold that picture?' He said, 'Till next Tuesday at the latest.' I said, 'Well, you hold it and I'll be there Monday and talk with the man who brought it in, the movie-maker.' You see, I happened to know that man; we're sort of friendly. And the attorney doesn't know him except on a business basis. So, about an hour after I was through talking to him, he withdrew the picture.

He said he's going to send it to New York, I think. A gentlemen's agreement between him and me that did what I wanted and got the attorney off the hook.

". . . It was awful. Came in three parts and had to do with prostitution and stuff of that sort. Besides, there was a terrible rape scene in the first part where two white men raped a dark girl. And I said that, to me, it would be foolish for us to let a thing, a picture like that pass for licensing, considering the racial tension in Baltimore. It was absolutely obscene anyway and I would never lend my name to licensing that particular film. The next segment was merely about a procurer, in other words a fellow who procured men for women. The third part was about a housewife who sort of went on the rocks. And, my, those last two were bad enough. But the first sequence was really terrible."

His voice lowered discreetly. "And this is why I'm so happy to have squelched it before it even got to the courts which might have let it by. And that white and black rape thing, it was bad. Terrible."

Could it have portrayed any trace of remorse in the hearts of the two white men who had raped the black girl? Could the film have been an attempt—even a slight one—to depict the hostility between the races? Could there have been some importance, some social significance in the rape, by showing white men's traditional attitudes toward black women?

After some deliberation, he answered. "It was terrible, disgusting—that's all. Such filth can't have social

26

significance, no matter what it's about. Such filth *can't have social significance.* It's pure dirt and you can't make anything moral out of *that.*

"But in view of those recent Supreme Court decisions —according to what the lawyer said—we'd have had to have licensed that if the producer hadn't decided to take it out of Maryland. And there's the bad part again about what the Supreme Court did to us. If the distributor of that picture didn't happen to feel friendly to me there would be nothing the committee could do. So you can say I had to use my personal pull with a distributor to get around the Supreme Court and keep such trash out of this state."

Mr. Quinn smiled again. "So, as this proves, some of us like myself, if the Court wouldn't go along and the sequence is bad—really bad—*I have ways to take care of it, all right,* and to protect the children in the neighborhoods from such dirt. The Court's not *all* that matters. The people and what they want—they're important too. If something's really bad and the board's overruled on it, I plan to get as many family groups, PTA groups, neighborhood groups, church groups that's possibly interested in cleaning up some of these pictures. And to get them vocal and active. We had, over in Washington here, an example of that in a theater which was in a darky shopping center." His use of the word "darky" was not malicious; he used it constantly to refer to black people. "The theater was right where the darky kids had to pass on their way to school and all. And the signs advertising the pictures were just terrible. And the people got together and did OK in having them removed. We helped them with advice.

"Then, the same thing happened over here in Baltimore, strange to say, also in the darky section with terrible advertising and all. And, by golly, those neighbors had a lot of action. They got together down there and they went down and told the manager that if he didn't take the advertising signs down, they would. So he took them down, and I had him come down to the office and he told me, he promised that would be the last time.

"And over in another section—a white section—some time back, they were showing and advertising dirty pictures. And the neighbors got together and they waited on the movie house there that was showing one of these awfully dirty films and they got the manager to stop showing the film. So I mean neighborhood groups can do a great deal if they will.

"But don't think I haven't been criticized by people for what I'm doing. Newspapers like the Washington *Post* and the Baltimore *Sun* have written bad articles about me for not wanting to see dirt around this town. But I'll take all the publicity I can get, no matter how it makes me seem to some people. Because that's more important than me or anybody else on that board. That's *youth* I'm talking about protecting and they're the ones that count.

"A while back an article appeared in the paper saying that right here in Maryland there were more than a thousand teen-age girls pregnant. Imagine, there were a thousand they knew about. How many were there that they didn't know about? Facts like these disturb me. Maybe I shouldn't get so worked up, but when people's morals get as loose as the morals of the American people are apparently getting and the movies show it, then we're in really serious danger in this country of losing something that we can never get back again.

"I think the danger in this country is growing every day. Maybe I'm crazy. You know, 'All the world is peculiar except me and thee and thee is peculiar at times.' Maybe it's me. But I mean I don't think anything takes the place of decency and morality in a family, in a community, in a city, in a state or in the nation. And when you lose those things, I don't think you have a whole lot left. That's why there ought to be more boards like ours instead of all this silly stuff about getting rid of ours. For the sake of morality and the family."

The first thing you must note about Mrs. Mary Avara, Mr. Quinn's "most valuable" committee member, is her overflowing vitality. She is a tall, slightly stoutish woman with a kind, jolly face, a pleasant, husky voice, liquid brown eyes and the movement and authority of a woman who knows what she is about. Her earliest conversation reveals her to be as benevolent as she looks and very earnest about people and things, especially the Maryland censor board. Mrs. Avara believes passionately in God and people's inherent good . . . when guided in the right direction.

She talks about herself without inhibition, and with a staccato excitement. "Well, I was born and raised in West

Baltimore. My mother had eighteen children. She raised twelve boys and six girls. Everybody loved her. She loved people and she loved all us children and showed it and none of us ever gave her any trouble whatsoever. Because no matter how much she loved us, she always ruled us with an iron hand. We all obeyed my mother; we obeyed her till the day she died. We never, at any any time, answered my mother back in any way, shape or form, and we were happy.

"My mother was very religious and we all went to church every Sunday. We led a good sheltered life." Her voice rises. "And we didn't know everything about sex like the ones today. I don't mean just when we were very young. Now they know things at four and five. Not us.

"As we grew older, we still didn't know anything. I remember one day, I asked my mother where chickens come from. I got a beating because she said, 'I will tell you when the time comes.' She didn't want anybody to put any ideas in my head. And at no time did we ever say to my mother, 'Are you going to have a baby,' like they do today.

"We would get up in the morning—my father would have the coffee made and my mother worshiped the ground my father walked on. My mother thought—she must have thought sex was beautiful—with eighteen children. But at no time did I ever hear my father say anything that was dirty, in any way, shape or form. Never! We never saw my father kiss my mother. Never!"

Mrs. Avara married a very handsome man from Italy,

who "looked like Cesar Romero, exactly." His most profound ambition was to become an American citizen. He was killed in an automobile accident before he could do so, though.

"It was right before Christmas, you know; he was buried on Christmas Eve. And we had put the wreath in the window. And the tree was up. And my children didn't understand. Their toys were upstairs. They were only three, five, seven and eleven. And they didn't understand why this Christmas wasn't cheerful and where their father was. And then, after my husband died, we found that the insurance company where he had insurance had gone up in the hands of receivers. But we went to court and I received, I think, a forty thousand dollar judgment on his life. A piece of paper."

She sighs, recalling that day in the courtroom, but talks about the courage God gave her.

"Well, you can't feed your children on paper. So, I know the bail-bond business. I used to work at it to help out before I was married. So I figured I'll go back to that. And I'll pray. I told myself all these things. So I didn't cry but I went down to about a hundred and eleven pounds. And I worked and kept going to church. I got on my knees every night and prayed for my children. I'll tell you, I got to a point I thought God was going to take all my children. I slept in one room with all four children. And I started going to station houses only when the children were in school. But I took my littlest girl with me."

The nuns in St. Peter's, the church Mrs. Avara and all

her children still attend regularly, kept her three older children while she worked. And, finally, her hard work paid off; a man asked her to become his partner in the bail-bond business. "And I never let him down, worked every day and never went out of the city of Baltimore, never took a vacation until my Cetta, my baby, was fourteen—eleven years. I didn't leave the city. And then one time, the Democrats had a convention in Chicago and my young son and my little girl, Cetta, wanted to go, so we went. Cetta was very, very religious. All the way while we were traveling, she kept looking up at the clouds. I said, 'Cetta, why do you look up there?' She said, 'Mom, what would you think if I told you someday I'm going to be an angel up there?' Sam, my boy, said, 'The only angel you will be is in St. Peter's church plays.' She said, 'Never you mind, Sam, because I will. I will someday. And I'll sing. And when I sing in heaven, Mommy will be real proud of me.'

"So, on August fifteenth, the Holy Day of Obligation, we were in Chicago. August fifteenth. And when we came home, August twenty-second, my baby, Cetta, was killed by a car. . . . She never knew whatever hit her because she was knocked unconscious immediately."

In the hospital, Mrs. Avara said, she sat in the dreary waiting room and kept rubbing her cold arms, praying: "Don't take her. Dear Jesus, don't take her." Suddenly she felt a fatherly hand on her shoulder. It was Cetta's doctor. "He said, 'Mrs. Avara, would you want your daughter to be an imbecile or would you want the Lord to take her?' I said, 'She's so proud. I hate to say this, dear

God. You should say, "Thy will be done." ' I said, 'Thy will be done, but I'll bet God's going to take her.' And with that, the door opened and the nurse came in and said, 'Your daughter has passed away.'

"And now she's in Heaven and she's always interceding for me. She said she would and she does. And I thought I would die after she did, but I didn't. You work, you pray—you just ask God to give you strength. You can't just go around thinking. And you help other people."

Almost from the day she married, Mrs. Avara had organized and serviced elderly women's clubs and had done other charitable work, which makes her something of a political influence in her area. And she has worked in her church.

"So, after Cetta died, I didn't give up my activities. I'll never forget, a judge I knew from the bail-bond business said, 'You're so brave, nothing can get you down.' He said, '*People need you.*' The priests would talk to me the same way and the sisters. They were so much help to me. Any denomination—anybody I talked to regardless of denomination—they were always saying, 'Oh, you know that the people need you.' "

Mrs. Avara was appointed to the movie censor board in 1960. The first movie she saw was *Crack in the Mirror*. Owing to the fact that she had lived such a good life at home with her parents, "never seen something dirty," it shocked her. Out of all proportion, she admits now, because comparing it with what she has seen since, "It was nothing so dirty. But I thought it was terrible. It wasn't bad, really, it was about a woman having a love affair with a man and her little girl sleeping in the next room. I thought, if you should have a love affair, you shouldn't have it in the house where your little girl was. I carried on like a maniac.

"Little did I dream how the other world lived, you know. And after going to the Court of Appeals on different films that came into the office here and getting turned down, you just think—well, I walk outside and expect to find people walking around nude. You testify. You go to court and they say, 'You have to have expert testimony.' Why do you have to have expert testimony? I think being a mother's enough.

"I'd just like to be able to do something. But where are we going to start and how? Based on the decisions from the Court of Appeals, our hands are tied. They're so—like *A Stranger Knocks*—I thought that was terrible! And the *D Girls*—about a woman who had a husband who really wasn't satisfying her. You'd have to see it to know how awful it is. Even if I am fifty-six years old, it's a good thing it's dark back there in the screening room because I get so ashamed. Dear God! If this isn't terrible. The morals getting so low, and I remember my father told me—all these sayings come to me, that when the morals of the people get low, it's a sign the country is going to pot. He would say that in Italian."

She returns again to *A Stranger Knocks*. "The woman in it was terrible . . . Well, there was a man who ran away from some prison there and he had an affair with her and she took him home. It was a story, I guess, and that's what the Court says is necessary. But it was—really —I mean, they leave nothing to your imagination. Nothing whatsoever. You'd have to see these films that we look at all the time in order to know what we mean. I just get sick all over. I think this job was a wonderful job years ago, but it seems, since I've been on the board, it's oh, things are *so* bad.

"Well, now—here lately you get three and four terrible movies at a time; and they're shown in neighborhood theaters. And they used to show good movies. Now, it's all that dirt. Movies here charge a two-dollar admission fee and they say that keeps the children out. But what people don't know is that if a person— sometimes a twelve- or fourteen-year-old child looks older than their years and has got two dollars and the movie people are going to let them in. I mean it's just disgusting and there's no—we would just like to know how and where are we going to start to do something to stop everything."

Like Mr. Quinn, Mrs. Avara thinks community action may be an answer. But she is not as certain as he that there are enough people with a sense of community responsibility to make a difference.

"I mean, if we can just get the community to think, but we can't. I mean how do you know where your children are? You can't follow them; you can't tell them you don't trust them. But they may be there seeing some of those terrible things."

Mrs. Avara is talking of other people's children. She has no worry over her own. Like her, they have a sense of values and are perhaps even more repelled than she by some of the films, even though they are "all grown now." She says:

"My son always said, 'Mom, let me come to a showing.' My older son who is very religious. He came and he looked at half of one of our films and went right to confession. He never wanted to come again. My daughter asked too, so I brought her. She said, 'I'm sorry I asked you.' She walked out before the picture was half over. And my other son, the youngest boy, came with me once. He's six foot two, handsome, looks exactly like my husband. And after he watched a picture, he went into the men's room and upchucked. He told me, 'Mom, that's terrible! I never thought a picture could be that bad.' And that's a boy twenty-seven years old."

Mrs. Avara admits herself to be a Walt Disney fan. "I love those pictures, too, and some even with sex in them if it's clean.

"I read this law book on obscenity. I read it through and through. It says if there's sex, but the story still has a plot to it, you have to consider the picture as a whole. Now take a picture like *Irma La Douce*. I considered that picture as a whole and I thought it was cute. Because by the time your sex is aroused you've laughed and so it's good. I thought that was a good picture. But what's the use of me studying this book when it isn't even clear and says a picture's all right if it arouses sex as long as it's art.

"All right, my father loved art. He loved art paintings of beautiful bodies. But you see these people in these

films; that's not art. My father wouldn't call that art
and who would say that art isn't appreciated in Italy?
My father and my mother both talked about art. Who
loved a beautiful woman more than my father? He
would say about a picture of a beautiful woman, 'Isn't
that beautiful? *That's* art.'

"It's terrible, the movies coming out that we on the
board have to see. I mean you really have to see in order
to believe what we go through. I get in here to my
office every morning and I'm so nervous. I never was so
nervous in my life as since I took this job. I come in in
the morning and I hope we don't have a picture today.
Sometimes they come three at a time and I can't even
remember the names of them anymore.

"My mother would always say 'Sex is beautiful!' And
those movie people make a mockery of it. That's a disgrace. It's a sin and a shame. The filth, the filth and the
garbage; utter garbage. It's a disgrace. Why, the state
of Maryland really and truly should be proud that we're
the only state with a movie censorship board. We're
trying to fight to keep decency in the state. But how many
people will go along with you? How many people do you
find that want to go get a petition? My people—*my* kind
of people, simple, never went beyond eighth grade like
me—*they're* complaining. They're the ones who'll
come and say, 'Gee, Miss Mary, you ought to see what's
showing at the movie.' Do you know that? Now that's
my low-class uneducated people. They're no experts.
Only people that know dirt when they see it.

"But you do have people that actually are a little more

37

worried here lately than ever. We've got all kinds of calls now. Recently. People say: 'How did you ever pass this picture? How did you pass that one?' They don't know about the courts having us tied."

Mrs. Avara drums her fingers on her desk and says: "*Lady Chatterley's Lover* was shown in the Baltimore theaters. I wasn't on the board then but it was released after the committee took it to court. And some of these other pictures they show on East Baltimore Street with naked bodies right out in the open where our children can see them. Believe me, they're even worse than *Lady Chatterley's Lover*. I don't know how anybody can go in a movie on East Baltimore Street and see the pictures there and not say 'Pictures like these they show on this street for children to see. That's what this country's coming to!' It's like my father always said when he was alive . . . no morals, we're going to pot."

II

Poor Men's Grindies—the Tamest Pornographic Movies Made in America

THOSE children who can be found on the East Baltimore Streets of America, the skid rows from New York to San Francisco where the poor men's pornographic bookshops as well as movie houses abound, are far from the innocent young boys and girls Mary Avara describes. The few girls from fourteen to eighteen usually are prostitutes, infinitely more hardened than the older girls in their business. And the boys in leather boots and tight jeans to emphasize animal virility are here often with a sinister purpose: to prey upon homosexuals or other men.

No matter how gaudily a skid-row "grindie" movie proclaims its program of the day, a line in front is unheard of in any city—New York, Los Angeles, San Francisco. In fair weather or foul, the poor men's pornographic theater audiences, including those who come only to drowse or sleep, seldom exceed forty or fifty customers at any given time. And some of these are homeless men who sit through showing after showing not because they are titillated but because they have no other place in which to spend their long, lonely hours. There are those who say, as does the writer for the book called *The Smut-rakers* and published by *Newsbook—the National Observer,* that "whether one attends a grindhouse in New York's tawdry Times Square or the downtown sections of Canton, Ohio, the atmosphere is always the same."

I have found different atmospheres in two grindie houses in the same city, to say nothing of the difference in cities like New York, Baltimore and Cleveland.

In New York, I went to one grindhouse paying three dollars for the privilege—grindhouse prices are not cheap—that smelled like a Bowery flophouse, pungent with the odor not only of plain, unwashed manhood but also of urine lingering in the air. In Washington, D.C., I attended a grindhouse for two dollars and seventy-five cents that, aside from its gaudy outside signs announcing unalloyed enchantment on the inside and picturing seductive girls, looked like any lower-class neighborhood movie house. And in Cleveland, for the same price, I went to a grindhouse that looked like a fairly prosperous middle-class movie.

Many grindie customers are skid-rowers who can become inflamed by movies that would leave most ordinary men accustomed to the sight of unclothed female bodies and to intercourse with women not only untitillated but bored out of patience after the first couple of sequences.

Others who do not live on skid row are recluses all the same. Some can afford to go to bars featuring live girls in various states of undress, but as is often the case with sexual recluses, live shows not only would interfere with their need for anonymity while indulging voyeuristic tendencies but with their tendency to fantasize while watching the girls. Also, those who wish can often masturbate in grindies as they cannot in bars or night-clubs that feature live shows.

Grindie movies, particularly those shown in cities with large skid rows, are often no more than scenes (*in color,* emphasize the distributors) of men and women, taken at some nudist camp. Of course they are naked except for covered genitalia. There are no words, but the actors generally engage in some activity, playing volley-ball perhaps, or swimming and romping around a palmed pool. And there is almost always a disrobing scene of a pretty new recruit who strips only after much coaxing. And shyly, to the volleyball players' unalloyed happiness, she may join them on the field in the nude, or loll nude around the pool.

Fortunately, the customers whose erotic hungers are so easily inflamed by such inane fare couldn't care less that these movies have no plots. There is no dialogue except for a narrated story and, once in a while, some irrelevant music—the "Volga Boatman," say—played as a triumphal accompaniment to the timorous entry of the new nudist onto the volleyball court.

Skid-rowers and other lonely poor men may come to grindies not only to see nude women but because it is a welcome release from a sordid tenement room or flop-house. They arrive early, carrying paper bags with sandwiches and sometimes wine or liquor bottles. They may watch the show once, twice, three times, relaxing eventually into a semicomatose state. Sometimes cheap streetwalkers come looking for potential customers. Most of these are new to the racket, since the more experienced know there are few "tricks" in grindie houses.

Sometimes, too, there are customers from the suburbs or a rural community. These are almost invariably disappointed by the alluring advertisements and a few demand their money back from the house cashiers, who generally return it without a mutter. One slender Forty-Second Street cashier in her late fifties, with dyed-red sausage curls, an old-timer on "the street," says, "Most who leave before the show's done because they're rooked by the signs don't come out too mad and only a few ask for their dough back. A lot fewer than you'd expect." She emphasized, however, that she and most cashiers return the money of disappointed patrons "without no argument." "We don't want no fights with bruisers from the sticks."

The nudie-show grindies for the more substantial customers, those not homeless or recluses but easily titillated all the same, not only show nude women's bodies but have a plot of some sort and lines spoken by actors instead of a single narrator. Although more expensive to produce than the nudies, they are made at the lowest possible cost by opportunists who are geniuses at flattering their personnel.

Earl Jackson is a typical plot-grindie producer. A man with conventional good looks who used to be a bond salesman before "adopting my present profession," Earl works mostly out of Hollywood, and, on occasion, out of San Francisco or New York where unemployed actors, writers and technicians are "a dime a dozen. I have an advantage over the nudie producers in getting the actors and actresses who want to show their talents as well as their bare bodies. I go right along with them, telling them how smart they are and how my grindies'll lead to a good career for them. Like I say, 'Sure, if you act in a real story, the producer who sees you doesn't think of you as *just* a body the way you'd be in a straight nudie. And with your body, kid, no man'd forget *that* anyhow. So there you are. Any way you look at it, you got it made both ways for the future when you're acting for me.' And what's money when you got a great future at stake?"

In practically every plot grindie, as in the nudies themselves, "the naked body," Earl says, "*is* important, more important than anything. But, then, plot grindies also require action; the more violent the better. We're mad for murder scenes. And what we're really looking for but seldom get from a writer who'll work at our price (that breed comes high) is a murder script with mystery and suspense in it."

He smiles. "Still not forgetting the nude body. You see, most of the guys who come to our movies aren't like the ones who go to the straight nudies. They're not loners. Many are married. Some come to our flicks with other guys, not by themselves like the nudie customers. Some come on their nights off from the little women. And when these go back home, you know their wives are going to ask them about what movie they saw, what it was about. And so we've got to give them more than naked broads to talk about."

Earl says that plot grindies, unlike nudies, do best not in the large cities with their correspondingly large skid rows but rather in the smaller industrial cities.

"And the less swinging a town is, even if it's not got a lot of industry, the better the market for my kind of flick. Bethlehem, Pa.'s a good place because, while it's got plenty of industry, it's far from swinging. Baltimore's a lousy market on the other hand. Too many things to do in Baltimore and my movies are only one of them.

"Washington's a great market though; the greatest. It swings for some fellows but not the ones I'm talking about. And everybody wants to be respectable in Washington. So thank God for Ninth Street. It's not really a porny center but it does have arcades where entertainment's cheap and the poor bums go. Well, my clients are no bums I'll have you know; they don't like to mix with bums or be mistaken for one. Which is all to the good where I'm concerned. Because the cheapest plot grindie in Washington [and most cities, he could have added] costs two dollars and seventy-five cents. The fellow who's not working regularly—the bum—can't afford that tariff. So he goes to the arcades instead of the grindies. And my fellows don't have to mix with him."

The arcades, unlike the plot grindies shown in two-seventy-five houses, are within range of the poor man's pocketbook—forty cents for a ten-minute black and white film and one dollar for a ten-minute color film.

"And the beauty of the whole thing," one arcade patron says, "is that you can see *something* even if you ain't got a dollar or forty cents."

The arcade film, usually emphasizing a pretty girl in negligee, high-heeled shoes and black underwear she may or may not wiggle out of before the piece is done, comes in four parts. You pay a dime for each black and white sequence and a quarter for each one in color.

A typical grindie plot is entitled *I Am a Bad Girl* and deals with the dissolute and unhappy life of a young girl seeking a career as a New York model. And what trials and tribulations she experiences! No matter what assignment she seeks—showing clothes, posing as a housewife in love with a certain wallpaper, paint or upholstery, she is told to remove everything she is wearing, down to black lace bra and panties. Even during her first assignment, when she is supposedly in discord over becoming "a bad girl," she strips in the grand manner of a duchess while whining pitifully about wanting to "remain good."

Once she is stripped, the photographer or manager invites her to sit on his lap, paws her so clumsily that any ordinary woman would be revolted, pulls down her brassiere strap, fondles her breast or perhaps kisses it—and the action is over. She remains sitting on the man's lap until he says she can get dressed. "You're a very lovely girl."

"But do I have the job?"

"I don't know, I have several more girls to interview before I make my decision." He almost pushes the girl off his lap; and still in panties and bra, she carries her dress over her arm into a second room where other models are waiting.

One, wrapped in a towel with nothing underneath except genitalia covering, joins the man in the outside room and experiences practically the same treatment. The mandatory scenes occur and recur for better than an hour and a half of testing of prospective models. (The audience, incidentally, never learns or seems to care which lucky miss gets the coveted job!)

"This is the picture the fellows *don't* tell their wives about," Earl laughs. "Now here's the one they do because, in addition to nudity, it's got mystery, murder, *everything*. And, besides, the woman wins the game. It's called, *Take Her by Surprise*."

The cast of *Take Her by Surprise* includes a businessman, who can, at least, achieve changing facial expressions, and his secretary whom he adores and wants to marry though he is already married. The wife, by the way, is of such profile and proportion one wonders why the businessman should reject her for the rather ordinary secretary. The picture also features a lascivious-looking hypnotist, curled black moustache and all, and an ex-convict who looks like nothing so much as a lion tamer.

The faithless husband, who dreams of ridding himself

of the wife, but tidily so the deed can never be traced to him, makes contact with the hypnotist.

"How would you like to earn five thousand dollars?" he says with a wink. *"In a short time?"*

"I would like to," falters the hypnotist. (Dialogue is never a strong point in such films.) "But what must I do?"

The businessman lays a reassuring hand upon the hypnotist's shoulder and says casually, "Not much, really. Merely hypnotize a man to murder my wife."

At first the hypnotist is shocked by the word "murder" but soon recovers when the businessman raises his offer to ten thousand dollars, and he agrees to take the job.

After he concludes his deal, the businessman goes home to his luxurious apartment. His wife meets him at the door in a nightgown like a ballet costume and golden high-heeled slippers. Although the men in the audience are visibly affected by the wife's loveliness, the husband regards her with insolence and displeasure.

They are shown at dinner in the living room and at last the wife invites the businessman to "accompany" her to bed. Dutifully, though unwillingly, he does so. Against her better judgment (you know she has tried in vain many times before) she lowers her nightgown to reveal a shapely breast and grasps at her husband, begging him to make love to her.

When he refuses, she cries, "This is it; the end. Now, I *demand* a divorce." He shrills at her, "What you want is a big share of my money. And you aren't going to

get it." Suddenly, though, he remembers that, come tomorrow, all the unpleasantness will be over. All he need
do is to distract the wife for another night. He tries to
soften her by embracing her, but he dislikes her so much
that he cannot even follow through. However, he knows
another way to reach her; he plays up his pity, penitence
and the regeneration of his love for her who has done so
much for him, and says he wants them to start their new
"love affair." But not in this apartment, an abomination
owing to the grief he has given her here, but in her favorite place in the world—their home by the sea.

Cut to the house by the sea. There are lovely views of
the wife, who has preceded her husband, sunning and
ocean-bathing in the nude. And there are sights of the
hypnotized convict, the potential killer, skulking around,
gun in hand, but entranced by his victim. You know from
his face, he would rather rape than kill her. Suspense. Will
the convict kill the wife? Or will he rape her?

Night comes—the husband has not arrived—and the
wife goes to her bedroom and undresses. Again, a long
scene of her in the nude, gazing into a full-length mirror, broken-hearted because her husband isn't with her.
Finally, she dresses in a flimsy nightgown and goes to
bed.

Enter the hypnotized convict, still carrying his gun
and still looking at the wife with vast desire. Again the
suspense. Will he rape her or kill her?

Answer! The convict flings away his gun, throws off his
shirt to reveal a virile chest, hurls himself upon the wife,
tears her nightgown partly off and showers her upper body

with kisses. She, frail though she appears, manages to throw him off and escape. She runs out of the house and into the woods. He follows, crazed. She keeps running. Now she is back in the house in her bedroom. He catches up with her before she can lock her door, grabs her again, hurls her on the floor and is about to rape her when she wrenches his gun from him and shoots him.

Now it is morning again, and the husband, accompanied by a witness, arrives.

"Darling," he cries out, expecting no answer. "Darling, I'm home. Where are you?" Sure enough, there is no reply. He acts concerned for the witness. "What could have happened to her? She knew I was coming and nothing—nothing could have kept her away—*unless* . . ." He cannot face his thoughts. "She must be dead," the husband says at last, but loud enough for the witness to hear clearly. "And I loved her so much."

"You're the greatest liar in creation," says a sharp voice. It is his wife, speaking from upstairs.

"Darling, it's you! You're here! You aren't dead!"

"I would be if you'd had anything to do with it." The wife runs down the stairs, shoots her husband, and tells the witness her whole story. He tenderly places an arm around her shoulder, covered with the half-torn Alençon-trimmed nightgown. "You poor darling," he says. "You can count on me to stand by you, no matter what happens."

No fool he!

"So," Earl Jackson smiles, "that's the kind of humbug I get good money for putting out; good money and a scurvy reputation. We grindie men are supposed to dream up the sexiest and most stimulating movies around. That's farcical, you know, when you consider some of the foreign flicks with their tremendous actors and productions that cost money so they really can make you flip. *And do.* If we ever tried to put art film sex scenes on the screen, I swear we'd be lynched.

"And why should we try? All we're interested in is making money and we've got enough customers who'll pay for what we've got without trimmings, so we don't have to be hifalutin.

"We know the customers we're catering to and we please them within our limitations. And the nice thing is we don't kid each other because we don't try to kid our customers. We're not competing. There're enough audiences to go around for all of us. Men—and some women —come because they want to, and our prices, though not cheap, aren't expensive either. So we can afford to be honest, well, fairly honest, with our customers as well as ourselves."

III

The Cherry Blossom Queen of Charlevoix, Michigan

I AM in a large bed-sitting room with kitchenette attached and containing only a large double divan bed, some armchairs, a table, bookcase and chest of drawers. None of this is expensive, but the paint is fresh and the carpet attractive, and there are prints on the walls of hunters in red coats taking fences boldly, and packs of dogs following lady riders with long veils floating from top hats.

John Custis and William Green, grindie movie-makers who, like Earl Jackson, work mostly out of Hollywood and for the same basic reason he does, that of economy, are making a movie, *I Can't Ever Go Home Anymore,* another version of *I Am a Bad Girl.* Custis is a tall, lanky man in his late forties or early fifties, with cold blue eyes and red hair streaked with gray that looks as though it hasn't been combed in days. More than anything else, he smells of the kind of liquid soap used in public washrooms. Green, also tall and lanky, wears a red shirt and tight blue jeans like a teen-ager. At first sight there is something boyish about him, rather naïve, until you realize he too is in his mid-forties, much too old for the image of flaming youth he is trying to project.

John Custis and William Green, like the majority of Hollywood photographers who are far and away the best technicians in the business, have on occasion done free-lance still photography for the major studios. With great pride, they show their scrapbooks containing still pictures shot on the sets and featuring Doris Day, Debbie Reynolds, and many lesser-known actors and actresses.

Enter a girl with cameo-pink skin and large blue eyes set off by dark lashes under a fluffed-out pineapple of light brown hair, the kind of a girl who brings to mind such clichés as "flower" and "rosy apple" and "Georgia peach." Smiling diffidently and speaking in a stilted way, Rowena Kane says she is twenty-one and had won a beauty contest in Scranton, Pennsylvania, four years earlier.

"Winning that contest meant *so much* to me. It was one of the loveliest things in my life; it really was. And now it's four whole years from the time I won that contest." She holds out both arms to embrace the passing of time. "I just never thought back then that it would be now and I'd be twenty-one instead of seventeen and have gotten a Hollywood contract but never be given a chance at playing a movie role. And Mama bragging about me all over town! I get so depressed, sometimes, I just sit home alone for hours and cry my heart out till I look like an old hag of thirty."

Five minutes after Rowena appeared, like a real-life version of *I Am a Bad Girl,* other models ("actors" and "actresses") troop into the room. Troy, a handsome Australian of twenty-six with wavy black hair and sun-bronzed skin, Rufus, six foot three and over two hundred pounds, with blond curly hair and chiseled classical good looks. And Ervie, no cute little doll like Rowena but a beauty entirely outside of the Hollywood mold, big and voluptuous and red-haired. Her skin is tanned and pulled tight against her face, revealing an exquisite bone structure. Her eyes are dark and restless, with large, shiny pupils. She leaves her eyebrows pretty much alone and, oddly, her fingernails are unpolished and cut short.

Everyone, obviously, has been photographed before by John and William and it is remarkable how routine this business of posing seems to have become. Some, like Troy and Rufus, study their bodies and each other's, making comparisons as rivals. Out of their clothes, they parade like peacocks and approach the camera with self-satisfaction. Rowena, opening and shutting her large eyes, minces and rotates her hips through a dozen poses. Her head is tilted so that small gold tassels tremble from antique gold earrings, her only item of apparel except for genitalia coverings. With a ballerina's grace she shows herself on tiptoe and then off. Voluptuously, she flaps a powder puff against her back and breasts. She stands before a full-length mirror, regarding herself with affection. Then she kisses herself inside her inner arm, letting her lips graze the flesh.

Ervie's nude body is exquisite and she assumes proper

53

poses for accenting her voluptuousness. She caresses her breasts with a massagelike motion, first the right one, then the left, and finally both. Unlike the others she seems, even while posing, to be laughing at herself. After the camera stops focusing on her she slaps both breasts playfully but hard. Finally, the shooting done, John warmly congratulates the entire cast but signals Rowena out for special approbation. "You're a doll, Ro, a great little trooper, sweetie . . ."

"I swear I'm learning so much from you and Bill, I'll be able to use it in a film the homefolks'll see some day."

"Well, kid," John says heartily, "we're glad if that's true. But you know how it is—the best photog in the world couldn't teach you if you weren't a quick learner like you are and a hell of a good little actress even if you didn't get the breaks yet. But you will, doll, if you hold on long enough and don't give up."

"Do you believe all that?" Rowena asks. "Really?"

Dutifully, as though he has ministered to Rowena many times before in this fashion, John crosses his heart. "May God strike me dead if I don't believe every word I'm saying."

William watches him. "If *I* don't believe every word he's saying, may God strike my *mother-in-law* dead. And everyone *knows* how I love my mother-in-law." But he whispers his witticism so his actors won't hear. And when Rowena asks whether he agrees with John, he says that she can bet her "cute little ass" on his faith and confidence in her and "all the other kids. In the meantime, all you got to do is stick with Bill and me. The breaks'll come and everything you do here'll come in handy when they do."

"Mmm," Rowena says. "I try to learn everything people like you and Bill've got to teach me, John. And I pray to God for my chance."

Ervie scoffs at everyone in the room through Rowena. She says loudly, "In Hollywood, Ro, baby, everything comes to him who waits. And as one of our kindhearted teachers and sponsors here, either John or William— I can't remember which—told you they'll take care of us so long as we keep waiting and posing for their porny pictures. So what's to worry about? God'll lead us while John and William feed us. And if we wait till they're sick and tired of us, well, we'll have been eating till then anyway."

Nobody, Rowena least of all, heeds Ervie. William and John know the truth of their future better than anyone, but it is to their advantage to flatter their "actors" and so to keep them working, as Earl pointed out, satisfiedly and cheaply. For them, as for Earl, there is profit in stimulating the illusions they must live by if they are to last in this Hollywood. Rowena, for instance, would give up if she were not convinced some big star would somehow see these nearly nude pictures of her and be so impressed he would demand her as his leading lady. And Gina Lollobrigida would want Troy or Rufus for her movie lover.

Only Ervie knows better. Having lived through the Hollywood marathon for seven years, she knows that these pictures for an anonymous audience she doesn't even care to visualize may titillate but that they must be (and she along with them) as quickly forgotten as a dirty joke. When her job which will earn her two hundred and fifty dollars is done, she dresses in slacks, sweater, socks, mules. She has no need, she says, to own any more than a few changes; her present life does not require her to wear exciting clothes, although when she first came to Hollywood and was not "the tough trollop I am today," she thought there was nothing more important to her and her career than a wardrobe. Now, though, she sees no prospect of ever having to wear feminine clothes again. She says that she forgot months, probably years ago, how to feel really feminine, though it would surprise the males who buy her nude photos and go to see "the ridiculous grindie films" she and other "Hollywood non-actors like us make."

"Oh, it's a great life I tell you, socially as well as every other way. God, I wish I'd never come here at all. And my mother, although she's got no notion, from me anyhow, of what I'm going through, feels the same way. Actually, of course, she was scared of having me come here in the first place."

Ervie's mother, she says, would have been just as happy if, instead of having been selected Cherry Blossom Queen of Charlevoix, Michigan, and ultimately Miss Michigan, she had married Mike Roberts who, at twenty-three, was already a partner with his father in the largest gas station in town. Ervie's mother had gone to school with Mike's mother, they had been bosom friends all their lives and thought the kids, too, ought to have a lot in common.

And, strangely enough, the kids did have a lot in common. "I loved being with him, having him touch me with affection. Yes, affection rather than sex. Just being in his arms made me happy. I'd never experienced anything like that before, not even as a child. Oh, my mother gave me plenty of affection. But I couldn't feel secure with her even though I knew she'd do anything for me. As for the boys I knew, either they wanted to take me to bed or else they wanted to be seen with me. And my father, God, I've been afraid of him all my life."

Ervie's father, sarcastic and knife-edged, had a pointed chin and a razor of a mouth "that still bugs me when I think about him." He was a small-time farmer and an altogether insignificant little man who boiled with rage at his wife because he was aware that in the eyes of all the townspeople she had married beneath her; he would come home and "beat the hell" out of Ervie and her mother. Ervie's eyes fall shut as though scorched by a vision. "Well, now, *I've* gotten away from his beatings but my mother's still living with him. And she's proud. She'd do anything to keep her friends from finding out about her life with him. One thing I'd hoped to do if I made it here in Hollywood was to offer her a home with me." Ervie's hands with the short, unpolished nails lie open. She looks down into them like a palm reader.

"I know now I'll never be able to give Mom a home. That means she'll never live to get away from that bastard father of mine. That's the way the cookie crumbles, I guess. Something happens to make you think you've got it made, and all the time you don't. I even thought I could make it for my mother. It was partly that thought that made me forget about Mike and all the plans we'd had—it was like they'd just disappeared from my mind —after I became Charlevoix Cherry Blossom Queen and Miss Michigan and was offered a year's contract in Hollywood. I was eighteen and innocent as hell . . . I was so thrilled, so goddamned excited . . ."

Ervie's excitement did not just spring out of winning the beauty contest and securing the Hollywood offer. There were so many small surprises coincident upon having won. There were the three days she spent in Detroit before going to Hollywood when she found herself being constantly photographed: with the governor and the mayor, drinking in a cellar club, dining in a plush restaurant, dancing in a night spot on top of a skyscraper. Her table was decorated with red roses and she drank French champagne for the first time in her life. Her escort, a handsome young man whose name she can't remember anymore, was constantly leaping to his feet and toasting her while the cameras clicked. And two men in formal dress asked her escort's permission to drink to the Hollywood success of the most beautiful girl they had ever seen. Soon every unescorted man in the place was drinking to Ervie and her career.

The next morning her eyes were heavy and her head dull from lack of sleep, but she felt lighthearted as she rode in a black chauffeur-driven limousine to the department store which outfitted her with a complete new wardrobe worthy of a Hollywood star, a wardrobe such as she had never in her wildest dreams visualized herself owning. Even now, dressed in her customary slacks and sweater, she is ecstatic at the memory of the bathing suits, sports clothes, cocktail dresses and yellow, blue, pink and white debutante gowns that had been especially designed for her.

Ervie's three days in Detroit were "like celebrating all the Christmases of my life." Her parents and "half the town of Charlevoix" came to the airport in Detroit to send off the rising young star. Everyone crowded around Ervie, admiring her clothes, wanting to touch her and shake her hand. She was full of joy, hardly conscious of what was going on. She posed for more newspaper photographs with her parents and Mike.

"I felt like a princess or a queen when I got on the plane to California," she says, "someone out of a fairy tale. I knew life from then on would be wonderful; a complete change from what it had been. And my father would be sorry he'd treated me as he had. That was important to me; showing my father."

Sitting with Ervie for days and nights at a time, watching her drink whiskey as she does, it is hard to imagine how she can remain so lovely and so untouched—no lines, no droop of bitterness, no slackness of appearance and speech—after eight years in the terrible Hollywood of her experience, five lived as a near-alcoholic. She be-

59

gins drinking in the mornings and continues through the night, generally alone but with a date if she is "lucky enough to have one."

Hard, cynical, bitter—that's Ervie behind her lovely changeless façade. It is really extraordinary, she says in a low, thoughtful voice, how girls like her cling to the idea of remaining on and on in Hollywood, putting up with every sort of indignity imaginable (posing for pornographic pictures is not the worst thing she has had to do) and yet stubbornly refusing to give up and go home.

"Do you know something?" She taps a cigarette nervously. "I started sleeping with this assistant director when I first came to Hollywood. And he gave me the clap."

Ervie turns the glass round and round in her fingers, staring into it. "I'll tell you what I did about it. I got cured and then I slept with him again. I thought I had a good reason, too. Because just one year after all of the hullabaloo, all the stuff that happened in Detroit and everything, the studio dropped my contract. Just like that. All year after I came to Hollywood, I hung around and didn't get one lousy part in one stinking picture before the studio dropped my contract. I was so humiliated. And this guy, the one gave me the clap, said he'd have it renewed. That's the way he put it, too; right on the line. If I put out for him, he'd put out and get the studio to renew my contract. And he continued making promises like that, dangling a new contract, so long as we were together. I just drank the silly business down and went to bed with him again.

"He was repulsive to me, a smelly little redhead. He was *really* repulsive to me, but by then, I'd have slept with a gorilla if I'd thought he could help have my contract picked up again. So we'd talk about renewal and he'd put me off to next week, next month. And after six months of promises that came to nothing, I went to his house and raised hell. He smacked me around to shut me up and then told me to get out of his life; he'd had enough of me. It all ended up with me telling myself I can't let that contract slip out of my hands now after everything I did so far and begging him to forgive me for making a scene. So he let me back into his bed for a couple of weeks and then found a new girl, a small-town contest winner, naturally, who believed in him as I didn't anymore. Then one night, just like that, he told me he was through; he never wanted to see me again. And when I asked him about the contract, he looked at me like I was out of my head and said, 'Contract? What contract? Jesus, but you're a gullible broad.'

"Come to find out, he couldn't have had my contract renewed if he'd wanted to. I didn't know when I first met him that a lousy little assistant director has to take orders like everyone else. Assistant Director's just a crap title in Hollywood but it takes a new starlet a long time to realize a man's not Darryl Zanuck because he's got the words Assistant Director next to his name. Once I dug the deal, I had to use twice the amount of hooch to drown *that* disappointment down. Not only had I given up my cherry as my old man always predicted, but I'd gotten nothing out of it as he'd also lovingly warned. I was so ashamed, and I developed this terrible fear that my mother'd find out about the whole deal. That thought really knocked me out because, well, I was all that made her life worth living. And she's very strict about morals just like most Charlevoix women. If you come right down to it, I used to be what some girls would call a prude myself, believe it or not. I know I'd never have gone to bed, actually gone the whole way with any man except the one I married if I'd stayed home.

"The whole atmosphere of Hollywood's different though. You begin feeling that going to bed, especially with a fellow who'll advance your career (*you think*), is the smart thing to do and that you're a schmoe if you don't. It may take a while, but once you get here you forget the values you used to have. You begin to think of sex as not mattering, except as a little thing to sell for a role that may just make a star out of you."

The problem, however, as many unknown starlets soon discover, is that "your sex appeal that makes the hometown boys drool leaves the movie men cold. There's too much of it around and the girls are always throwing themselves at the men, especially if they think they can do something for them. Actually, most men girls like me, unknowns, get to meet couldn't help you even if they were so much in love with you they really wanted to. Most men we unknowns know are nobodies just like ourselves. Some of them pretend they're somebodies for a while like my redhead did, but they disillusion you soon enough.

"Oh, a few lucky kids catch the eye of somebody important and he wants to take them to bed or maybe even finds himself going for them, so he stakes them to a career, but those girls are the sports. They're accidents. I don't know any important men in Hollywood I could try to vamp into helping me, any more than my mother does. And I don't ever expect to meet any. This drinking of mine," Ervie goes on, "it's the only way I can keep going. I started drinking just a little bit when I hadn't been in Hollywood long, and I began to realize I just might not get where I'd thought I would, sex or no sex. I was still under contract at the time and so I was all right for money, but there wasn't anything to do except just to live through the days hoping for a call from the studio that never came. And the nights were worse than the days. I had nothing to do but sleep and I couldn't. So I started taking a couple of drinks before I went to bed to help me sleep. Then I had the idea of starting earlier than my bedtime, to pass the time and kill the loneliness and doubt.

"And finally I began drinking in the daytime too because I was just as lonely and doubted myself as much in the daytime as at night."

Why, then, since Ervie's past is a forewarning of the bleak future that lies ahead of her in Hollywood doesn't she return home? Her answer is more or less typical of that of most unsuccessful starlets, especially those who have reached Hollywood by way of the beauty-contest winners' road. Ervie, though to an infinitely lesser degree than most contest-winner Hollywood misfits, has no particular assets other than her good looks. And, again like most contest winners, she came to Hollywood from a small town and a basically deprived background. While some winners' mothers have, like Ervie's, hoped to find better futures in their beautiful daughters' successes, others have been jealous and hostile toward them. And if you must return home a failure, after having reveled in proving yourself a success to people you have always wanted to impress, it is hard to go back beaten unless you have toughness and resolution. Besides, to go back a loser to a small town is not like returning to a city where you can take up the threads of your old life or begin a new one, without being gossiped about. Also, Ervie asks, once you have seen Hollywood, once you have been exposed to the glamour, can you really conceive of yourself as the wife of a Charlevoix gas station owner, assuming that the man you loved will take you if he hasn't already married?

"It's a terrible thing to say but well, much as I loved Mike before I came to this hellhole, there was still something about it that made me believe my future lay in a better place than Charlevoix. So, call it crazy or anything you want, I wouldn't go home for anything."

In order to stay in Hollywood, therefore, Ervie and many of her down-and-out colleagues engage in activities that may repel them—posing for pornography, serving as expensive call girls, and when even these jobs are not available, waiting on tables and car-hopping. Many strangely—in view of their Puritan morality—shudder more at the latter than the former.

Ervie stands out most clearly from the others "in that

I no longer kid myself, while they do." They maintain (like Rowena) the myth that they will make it some day. Maybe tomorrow for all they know. On pornographic picture assignments, or while with customers they sometimes service as fifty- to one-hundred-dollar call girls, they wait for some miracle to end the emptiness. You see them night after night in the bars and hotel lounges, alone or with other girls like themselves, beautiful and open to the attentions of presentable males and as fascinated by what they think they see around them—their all-too-rare glimpses of Hollywood personalities who have made it—as if they had never left their homes in Georgia and Michigan and Wisconsin.

One time after an unsuccessful trip to a restaurant for the prime purpose of making a pickup and after spending all her money, a girl named Sally came into Ervie's room in the studio club when she was at her most depressed and, after hearing her story, offered her a way out.

"Listen," said Sally, "you and I are going to leave this dump and find an apartment, a nice private apartment, where we'll be able to use the john anytime we need to. And more than that, we'll be able to entertain people."

For two weeks before she and Sally and Eileen, another friend, found their apartment, Ervie could not talk on the telephone or meet an acquaintance, male or female, without inviting them to come see them in their new home.

"We really didn't want just anybody to come. You see, we thought of the apartment as a sort of a stepping-stone.

We counted on that apartment to help make our careers."

Actually, the people who came to the apartment for the parties and the intimate little dinners served by candlelight were not much different from those the girls had known while they still lived at the studio club—people they had met while they were under contract whose contracts had also expired, a couple of old friends from their hometowns who came to Hollywood, and a few men.

"We invited every man we thought could be of help to us, but there weren't many we could get—a couple of first, second and third assistant directors, a few cameramen who hardly ever showed up because even the stars are nice to the cameramen and they certainly don't need the likes of us.

"Most men who did come came for the free meals and the hope of a free lay if we got desperate enough. And we *were* desperate. Because after a while together, we found we really didn't like each other very much, that maybe all we had in common was that we were contest winners."

Ervie says the apartment "always had some queer boys in it—nice but in love with each other, not us." Decorators and set designers, a few overtly effeminate in their chitter-chatter but most of them unrecognizable except to the initiated few. And there were other men too: a couple of sustaining writers, for instance, with cash in their pockets, making them "decent escort possibilities." All of them, of course, had their shortcomings.

Del, one such man, had a hair-cream ad handsomeness, six feet tall, well-built, young, blue-eyed and with wavy blond hair. "But he was on the make himself. He was looking for bigger fish than Eileen or Sally or me—a female star who could help him in her studio or a thirty-five- or forty-year-old woman or maybe somebody older who'd want a young man like him hanging around and so would take him under her wing. It's happened to guys like Del over the years; not very often, but it has happened."

While he waited for his big break, Del, like Ervie, worked at anything that came his way that was not "menial like waiting table." He, too, posed and still does for pornographic pictures and movies, and he "sleeps with older women for money. He's a male whore, you know, although he won't admit it. And the funny part of it all is he's not really a bad guy underneath. It's just Hollywood's done this to him.

"Not a bad guy." She laughs in a hollow, metallic way. "Listen to me saying he's not a bad guy. I guess that's like saying I'm not a bad girl." At twenty-five, she shakes her head to rid herself of what she labels her young memories; her young years, her young dreams, her young ambitions. "My life's over because I've done so many things I never thought I would and I hate myself for them. Well, if you don't like yourself, nobody else is going to like you either. And me, since after my first year in Hollywood, I think I stink."

She says what many observers of the starlet scene know. "Listen, those legitimates, the *way* they *use* us, are worse than William and John. I mean, sure William and John give us the business like they handed Rowena about how our pictures'll circulate in places where people'll see us and be overcome. I'd be an awful jerk if I didn't know (no matter what they say) that nobody's about to be overcome by any pictures I'd make for them.

"They ought to have a Society for the Protection of Beauty-Contest Winners in America. Take me. I'd never even *thought* of being an actress before they made me believe I could be one. I hate myself for having believed their silly lies. But I hate them more. Because, really, they're more to blame than anyone for the lousy life I'm leading now. I was a ninny but they were rotten liars for flattering me into believing I could be something I can't. And they gave me that one-year contract for one reason—I was good for a little publicity in the Michigan papers."

IV

"The Gorilla Won't Hurt You": The Tenderloin Kids of San Francisco

IT IS a cool August night in San Francisco and I am sitting with two homosexual hustlers, Gene Luv and Lee Lynch, on the stoop of Harvey Mann's house. Mann has been called San Francisco's foremost pornographic photographer. He lives on Bush Street near Grant in a strip called the Tenderloin—a blazing mixed bag of colors, Chinese, French and Japanese restaurants, jukebox bars catering to sailors in from San Diego and lesbian prostitutes, parking lots and garages filled with people going home after their night on the town. And the cheap tourist hotels.

Gene Luv has hustled men and sold drugs illegally since he was fourteen, but he looks chaste and innocent. Now twenty-two, he is tall, delicate and slender with curly jet-black hair, dazzling, large blue eyes and the kind of complexion women's facial creams advertise. He looks no more than eighteen or nineteen. Lee Lynch is also twenty-two but seems older. He has broad shoulders and looks virile, sturdy, lusty—the perfect male model.

Waiting with us on Mann's stoop are Joanie, Marilyn and Anise. Sometime-prostitutes, nightclub performers and models for nude photographs, they had been hired by Mann as actresses for a pornographic movie. Joanie, nineteen, looks entirely different tonight from when she worked as a topless dancer in Tipsy's Club—with her brash makeup and line of blarney to flatter the men customers so they would want to go home with her. Different, too, from the girl in dirty blue jeans with a fly front, her favorite apparel at home or on an LSD trip. But bare of makeup and clean tonight, her sad angel's face could come straight out of a confirmation photograph. She glances down at her watch and mutters with annoyance, "That cheap cunt Mann is always late. For all he pays us, you wouldn't think he'd have the gall to keep us waiting."

Anise, twenty-eight, short, plump, red-gold hair fluffed wild, says in a motherly, chiding tone, "Watch your language, honey." And Marilyn, twenty-two, a black girl with long, straight hair, the only one who has never been to college, pats Anise and says, "Ah, there's my sweet mama—always preaching to people about their English and all. There's my sweet little mother-fucker trying to keep us all on the straight and narrow."

After keeping us waiting for over an hour, Harvey Mann appeared. A middle-aged man with homburg, British raincoat and whiskey-ad face, he apologized for the delay. His expression was guarded, his smile buttery as he led the way to his studio apartment, five stories up.

Mann was proud of his studio. With its two projecting fireplaces, book-lined walls, Oriental rugs, pipes, cigarettes in an extraordinary onyx case, women's negligees of pink, blue and dark red chiffon, it was a place of splendid planned clutter.

Mann's furniture was varied. Heavy old Victorian pieces left him by his Boston grandmother. A grotesque Chinese red cabinet, a conversation piece with his collection of ivory hippopotamuses, teakwood monkeys and a gorilla with jade eyes. A window seat contained a gold-covered Bible, several books of East Indian poetry, old blues records and, in a place of honor, a few old Billie Holiday and Bessie Smith albums. On the window seat, too, were the coffee mugs Mann refilled with gin as soon as they were emptied, Benzedrine pills in candy dishes and marijuana cigarettes in cookie tins.

Lighting a weed from the butt of a Chesterfield he was smoking, Mann said, "I'm as different from other photogs as a Paul Klee from a George Bellows. Creative, you know, rather than repetitive." He turned to Joanie. "Right, baby?"

"Hmm," Joanie said apathetically. "You're hip."

"Not hip, little one. Original, inventive. Ingenious, a visionary, actually."

"Hip," Joanie repeated, still in an indifferent tone, "that's what you are."

"Well," Mann said, "you may be right at that. Hip, too. At least compared to all the other photogs in California. Other photogs in S.F. and even L.A. don't know the score; they don't know how to get the best out of their models. With them it's all work and their pictures show it, you know. Hell, to get good pictures you've got to get your kids involved in what they're doing, make them think some of your ideas are really theirs. And make the occasion social to get your actors in the right frame of mind. Use gin, bennies, weed, suggestion, auto-suggestion, psychology, what have you? Then talk the right words, plant positive thoughts about how it's kicks to go sexy in front of a camera. Never mention work at all. Tell people something's a lot of fun and you're fifty percent sold."

His voice dripped honey, like some huckster selling soap. But the camaraderie that had existed among the rest of us earlier, while waiting for Mann on the stoop outside, was gone. No one talked or smiled. Marilyn sat sulkily alone, Joan's eyes were closed. Anise drew doodles on a memo pad she had picked up in the studio somewhere, Gene balanced an unlighted cigarette on his upper lip. One by one, Mann examined the faces around the room. "Are you ready, kids?"

"I am," Gene said.

"Me too," Lee said.

Mann, his eyes needle-bright, said, "Let's go then." He put some dance music on the hi-fi and turned the volume up until the sound permeated the dim atmosphere. Anise and Lee, entirely nude, danced together. So did Joanie and Gene Luv. The space was so small and they gave themselves so completely to the beat that their dancing seemed more blatant than the overt sexual acts they would engage in later.

After ten minutes, Mann called a halt. He told Joanie

to stretch out on a rug. She has a pretty, if not particularly full-bosomed figure, and her legs, though long and graceful, bulge out at the calves and her ankles are not quite trim. Lee, at Mann's direction, stood above her, looking down at her body.

"Hey, you boy, look at Joanie as if you were in love with her," Mann said as he fussed with his lighting arrangements. "Give it passion, for Christ's sake, will you." Lee's "passion" was obviously simulated and Mann was dissatisfied. "Real passion, boy," he commands. "Make yourself look like you care. A kid like Joanie, it's not so tough. She's not exactly repulsive, you know. I tell you what, think of what you're going to do when you get down there on that carpet with her. OK, *get down.*

"Now, go on and get with it. Get on her, Lee. And Joanie, you fight him . . . OK, good. Good girl. Now, quit fighting. Quit struggling. Bring your hand up and touch his face and cling to him. Lee, kiss her ears and her neck. Kiss her all over and act like you're hung up on her breasts the way any square guy'd be if she laid for him.

"And you, Joanie, don't just lay there like a wooden doll. Remember, sweet, you're supposed to have hot pants for Lee, not act like he's not around. What's the matter with you kids tonight? Joanie's a block of wood and Lee, you look like you're in some kind of torture or something. Damn it, if you don't get that who-gives-a-damn expression off your face, I'll put you out of the picture."

Underneath his simulated expression of joy, Lee's expression was baffled and terribly young, with the harshness that comes from pain and fear. All the time he made love to Joanie, finally ending in complete intercourse, the bafflement and pain and fear were what you noticed most about him.

After Lee finished with Joanie, Gene got onto the rug with her. And then Lee and Gene together. While Joanie had oral intercourse with Lee, Gene had anal intercourse with Joanie. And never once was one as involved with the other as they had all been while dancing.

"Joanie, Lee, Gene." Mann stood alert after his warning to Lee, his eyes on his actors' faces. "You act like dumb bunnies who can't take simple direction."

"Sorry, Mann, but I'm tired tonight. Maybe I should've copped out on this one."

"Poor Joanie," Mann said. "All right, baby, we'll stop a while for cake and coffee." While everyone relaxed, quite comfortable in their nakedness, Mann made coffee and served it in elaborately fashioned cups on a tray with cloth and napkins embroidered with his full name. "Eat some of these cookies, kids. Food gives you strength." He clucked over them like an anxious mother.

Everyone sat around, eating cookies, drinking tea and engaging in teatime chatter as though at a party rather than the filming of a pornographic movie. And then the telephone rang. Mann answered it. "Harvey Mann here." He smoked a marijuana cigarette and listened. He said, finally, "No, don't you come here. I'll pick you up at your place and we'll straighten the details on the way back." Listening, the actors seemed frightened. Mann ignored their looks. "Sorry, kids, I'll have to leave you for a couple of minutes. Relax. Take it easy. As they say in old Mexico, '*Mi casa es su casa.*'"

Mann's few minutes stretched into half an hour. Joanie picked up a negligee lying beside her on the floor, the pink one, and wrapped herself in it. Lee poured gin for everyone. Anise clasped her hands over her bare chest and began to hum an old jazz number. Gene paced up and down the studio, looking like an ascetic saint in his nudity.

Mann returned finally in the company of a man of thirty-two or three, Hank La Matte. A huge man with a big chest thrust forward and swinging hairy hands he couldn't seem to control, he looked like nothing so much as an ape. And "Gorilla" was the name by which the others called him.

Immediately the mood in the room was changed. It throbbed with tension. People were no longer impersonally frightened; everyone straightened, stiffened.

"I won't do it again," Joanie said. "You couldn't make me, Mann. I'm telling you I won't play with the Gorilla."

"Me neither," Anise echoed.

"Joanie, Anise, listen." Mann was at his persuasive best. "The Gorilla won't hurt you this time. I promise on my word of honor. And you know me; when I say word of honor, it's not lightly like most people. I *mean* what I say. You can *trust* my word of honor because you can trust me."

"Why?" Joanie asked.

"Why what?"

"Why should we trust you or your goddamn word of honor?"

Mann appeared devastated by Joanie's question. He said, "You should trust me because of your past experience with me. You, especially, Joanie."

"I told you the last time I wouldn't do what you want me to with the Gorilla for all the money in the world. I meant it, Mann."

"Joanie, honey, this time everything'll be different. I promise."

"No."

"Stubborn girl. Keeps saying the same thing over and over again. Will you play for an extra twenty-five? An extra thirty-five?"

"No."

"Well, I tell you, Joanie, baby, much as I love you," Mann's voice became menacing, "and want to do my best to help you and Bill . . ."

"Just leave Bill out of this, OK?"

"Sure, OK, doll, if that's the way you want it. We'll talk about you then. What I'm saying is that if you don't go through the bit I want you to with the Gorilla, I won't need you to play at all . . . Ever. So?"

"So what?"

"What do you say?"

"No."

Mann dropped his threatening manner abruptly, and

leaned over Joanie's chair now, so close to her his breath touched her cheek. "I don't want to put you out; not *you*, baby," he said in the low tone of a man who believes a girl ripe for a proposition. "And I know you really trust me. So you'll play and bring home an extra thirty-five for being Daddy's good little girl."

"Shit," Joanie said, "OK. Count me in if you want. But if I'm as sick and get as hurt as last time, so help me, I'll see you get yours if it's the last thing I do."

The others, as Mann had known they would, took their cue from Joanie and went along.

Mann, overlooking their threats, set to work as though the earlier words had never been spoken. He readied everyone for the big scene with the Gorilla. He used Marilyn and Joanie in an oral scene with one another ("the black body on the white is photographically striking as hell," he said with professional pride) and Anise in the same oral-anal scene with Gene and Lee that Joanie had had with them earlier. After perhaps ten minutes, the Gorilla, wearing heavy boots and skin-tight leather pants and jacket, strode onto the set and, at Mann's specific directions, hit out at Gene and Lee, separating them from Anise.

"Hit him back, Gene," Mann ordered. "Go on, stand up to the Gorilla. Punch him. Twist his balls off."

Gene hit out at the Gorilla but there was no fierceness in him.

"Gorilla," Mann said. "Do what comes naturally. Act like you're going to kill him. Joanie and Marilyn, mind

77

your own business. Keep concentrating on each other. Don't mind the Gorilla. Come on, Gorilla. Give it to Gene good."

The Gorilla kicked Gene. Hard and realistically.

Mann flashed his approval. " 'Atta boy, Gorilla." And to Gene he said, "You can fall down on the floor like you've had enough. You're bushed, see?"

After Gene had fallen, the Gorilla turned his attention to Lee. With eyes half-closed by sweat that rolled in solid balls from his forehead and a hairy paw raised to wipe the perspiration from his face, he looked more than ever like his namesake. He struggled with Lee as he had with Gene until Lee also fell on the floor, looking more beaten and dejected than any derelict.

"Are you OK, boy dear?" Mann asked.

Lee sucked at his lips. "Oh, sure, I'm just fine."

Gene laughed dryly. "I'm fine too, Mann."

Anise, knowing herself to be the next victim, listened to this exchange and to Mann's directions to the Gorilla and her in mute terror. And she submitted, inertly, apathetically, to Mann's directions. She let Gorilla kick and beat her and only came briefly to life when he threw himself upon her and moved his body viciously against hers. A sensitive person, she would later talk in detail about her reactions as the Gorilla manhandled her. From the moment she looked up at him, she gave in to exhaustion so complete and at the same time so strangely satisfying that she didn't even feel the beating and kicks. Then, after a while, she began to *be* again, and

one part of her tried to speak out, tried to beg the Gorilla to stop. But words seemed beyond the power of her
tongue or mind.

It was four in the morning when the Gorilla finished
with Joanie. Then Marilyn took Joanie's place. In her
case, however, the situation was reversed. Dressed in a
pointed brassiere and semi-sheer, lace-trimmed panties
through which the lines of her garter belt were plainly
and provocatively visible, seamless stockings and black
patent leather pumps with four-inch needle-sharp heels,
it was she who tortured the Gorilla, now naked himself.
His ferocity vanished with his clothes. He knelt before
Marilyn, who sat in a thronelike chair, and looked at
her with doglike devotion. Actually, he was the only one
of Mann's actors who made an attempt to achieve "the
mood" Mann strove for. "Look at Marilyn as though you
only have eyes for her," Mann said. And when Mann
ordered him to kiss Marilyn's shoes, he did so worship-
fully. Marilyn kicked him with her pointed shoes and
walked on him with her sharp heels, driving them into
his arms, his chest and his stomach, and he looked ecstatic as Mann ordered.

At long last the movie was made, Mann's show was
finally over.

"How do you all want to be paid?" he asked. "Joanie?"

Joanie filled a cup with gin and drank it down. "Acid,
Mann, dear. I'd like to be on a trip right now."

"Anise?"

Anise touched her cup with the gin in it to her cheeks

and forehead, discarded it, found a marijuana cigarette. "Oh, I'll have acid too, Mann. Christ, you ought to know by now."

"Marilyn?"

"Oh, acid, Mann."

Mann smiled and asked the Gorilla, in costume and looking savage again.

"Money, Mann. *Dinero*. If you got green, you can buy your own acid."

Mann sharply reminded the Gorilla that if he persisted in demanding cash, he would receive a straight five hundred dollars. If he was paid in LSD, however, his profit doubled. The Gorilla was a fool, Mann snapped, to turn down a thousand dollars' worth of LSD for a mere five hundred in money.

But the Gorilla only smiled and said he knew the one thousand dollars' worth of LSD cost Mann, through his numerous contacts, only three hundred and sixty-eight dollars on the wholesale market. He understands why the others take it; they are "on the stuff." Mann metes it out in installments, and holding so much of it with him is "like having it in the bank." (Mann is scrupulously honest with the acid-heads when it comes to dispensing the drug they have earned.) But the Gorilla, thank the good Lord in his heaven, is not an acid-head and so he wants his five hundred straight, please.

Mann and the Gorilla, seated in opposite ends of the room, regarded each other suspiciously. Finally Mann said, "OK, dammit. I'll give you a check then."

"I don't want a check, Mann. I want cash. Like I said a dozen times already."

"And I said I'll give you a check, lover." Mann walked to a window and stood twirling the pull of one of the shades. "Take it or leave it."

"I'll take it," the Gorilla sighed.

To Mann's relief, both Gene and Lee preferred their payment in LSD.

Church bells, street noises and Mann's Swiss-made "talking clock" announcing 8 A.M. The studio looked revolting; the air smelled of marijuana, stale tobacco, gin, moldy orange peels from oranges Mann had been eating throughout the night, and perspiring bodies.

The Gorilla left and then Gene said he guessed he would take some acid back to his pad and make a "trip." He needs one after all that has transpired this night. Lee said he would do the same. But the three girls didn't want to go home; trip or not, their trips always turned out bum after the sour experience of making such a movie.

Inevitably, the conversation turned to why young people, particularly young girls, gravitate to the Tenderloin. Anise, Joanie and Marilyn are agreed that some shared weakness of character made them all succumb to becoming LSD or heroin addicts or alcoholics or prostitutes or homosexuals and eventual residents of the Tenderloin. But weakness is an umbrella word, after all; shared or not.

What is certain is that weakness alone will not serve to

drive a girl on to the Tenderloin: circumstance, environment and the influence of others all play major parts.

Marilyn's story of her descent to the Tenderloin began some fifteen years before she was born in 1929, when her future parents came to New York, along with hordes of other sharecroppers, the poorest people in the South. They were told that marvelous opportunities for advancement existed there and no "color problem." They were told that blacks lived in houses with electricity, running water and indoor toilets. They were told that their children would go to the same schools and have the same possibilities for making decent lives as white children. To the sharecroppers, New York was the promised land where they and their children could, at long last, lay their burdens down.

Instead what they found were dirty, uncared-for slum ghettoes and, basically, the same sunup to sundown working hours they had known down South—"only scrubbing floors instead of working in the cotton fields." Their disappointment and bitterness and hatred were colossal; and their children, like Marilyn, inherited the total sum of their feelings—fury and discontent that warped their souls and wills.

"Man," Marilyn says, "I ain't like these other chicks who were *turned* evil. I was *born* that way."

Marilyn was the sixth and youngest daughter of a Georgia sharecropper. "I never knew my old man," she says, "except for what my old lady told me about him."

'According to her mother, Marilyn's father was handsome and well-built, a good man while the family still lived down South before Marilyn was born. More than anyone else in her family, it was Marilyn's father who dreamed and schemed to come to Harlem. Before they came, Marilyn's mother told her, envious but well-wishing relatives raised as much money as they could get together and held a love feast; and Marilyn's father, delighted at finally having been able to achieve his great ambition, sang the spiritual "Hallelujah I'm on My Way to the Promised Land."

Marilyn's mother believes she glimpsed the beginning of her husband's destruction the day the entire family, all carrying his dream like a talisman, went hunting for "the big and fine" apartment they had envisioned back in Georgia and finally found a place for thirteen dollars a week that was at least as sordid in its way as their Georgia shack had been. The whole family had to sleep in one room, hanging blankets as partitions. The longed-for indoor toilet the family had talked so much about was in the hall, and the vaunted plumbing leaked so that water was always seeping through from the apartment above. And there were rats. Marilyn's father said they would only live there temporarily, but they were still there when Marilyn was born.

"Well, my father couldn't take the guff, you know," Marilyn says. "So he walked the hell out on us when I was three months old. Before that, he gave Ma hell anyway with his drinking and whoring around. She may have missed him in bed but she sure didn't miss him any other way because, I mean, all he ever was to her was another mouth to feed."

Marilyn's mother supported the family by doing housework. Marilyn remembers hearing about the Depression years when her mother frequented the Bronx slave market.

"The mother-fucking broads looking for houseworkers would come around to where Ma stood with other women wanting day work, competing for what jobs there were. And the broads'd feel their muscles before they'd decide which one of them to take home."

You can see the red-hot fury boil as Marilyn talks about her mother's experiences. Is it really strange that she should have ended up on the Tenderloin, she asks. Was this really worse than dozens of other insults dealt to black women every day? She asked herself that question when she was solicited, at fourteen, by a white madam who supplied young black girls to a primarily white clientele.

"I knew about ofay broads from my old lady," she says, "and I learned about ofay men by myself. It was a tough hustle in that house I worked. We had a bunch of dirty old men. I'll never forget this one jerk who said I was a dog and made me crawl over the floor before he could get his peter up. Then there was a filthy bastard who'd say, 'I can't break through with nobody but a little black bitch like you.' Oh, it was loverly, I can tell you.

"When I got to be seventeen, you know, the madam didn't want me anymore. I was too old for her damn choosy customers. So she recommended me to her sister in Frisco, which is how I got here in the first place. Well, the sister had the same kinds of queer customers, so I soon got to be too old for her house too. Which is how I first began walking the Tenderloin when I was nineteen. And I'll tell you something—after all that happened to me in the houses I worked, I can't feel so bad about shit-kicking on the street. The way I feel is that things have got to go up because they sure as hell can't go any further down than what they are already."

Strangely, not many young Tenderloin residents have come from backgrounds like Marilyn's. The majority, though they live out of a suitcase, have their roots in middle and upper middle-class America.

Joanie, for instance, although she scarcely communicates with her parents now, is the daughter of a prominent executive and a woman pictured frequently on the society pages. Recently, on her way to vacation in Hawaii Mrs. Ward decided to stop off in San Francisco to have a few hours with her "baby girl," whom she had not seen in over a year. She had sent a hurried telegram the night before, instructing Joanie to meet her plane.

Joanie handed me the telegram and implored me to have dinner with her and her mother. "God, I'll have to spend the whole afternoon alone with her. Maybe I can stand that, I don't know; but the whole evening is too much."

That evening in a restaurant where the price of our dinner for three would have fed Joanie and her lover, a black girl named Bill, for as many weeks, Mrs. Ward had a "simply gorgeous idea." Joanie should throw a few swimsuits and evening dresses into a bag and accompany her to Hawaii.

"Thank you just the same, Mother, but no."

"Why? It won't cost you a penny."

Joanie looked at me helplessly. During the whole past year since her father had thrown Joanie out because of her relationship with Bill, I knew her mother had never contacted her only daughter. Now she was inviting her on a trip as though nothing had happened.

"No," Joanie said again.

"You're crazy not to come," her mother said.

"All right then, Mother, I'm crazy."

Offended, Mrs. Ward rose and, swinging her hips provocatively for every man in the room, led the way out of the restaurant and back to her suite at the Saint Francis Hotel. There, the incident forgotten, she loaded Joanie with gifts, discards, but costly ones that would bring a good cash price when Joanie and Bill marketed them: a pearl evening bag, a ruby bracelet, diamond earrings she took from her own ears.

After leaving her mother's hotel suite, Joanie said, "I wouldn't go anyplace with her if my life depended on it. Besides, she didn't even bother to ask me about Bill or if we were still making it together."

Joanie's summer world, when she was a child, was warm and secure, thanks to dear black Emma who came every year for the two months Joanie's regular nurse went home to Scotland. School was forgotten. So were her problems with her parents—her father in the city and her chic mother off on an extended trip someplace. She adored Emma who coddled her as her Scotch nurse never did and dried the tears that hardly anyone else ever noticed. They spent their waking hours together, roaming the woods; on rainy days, at home, Emma told Joanie stories in the cozy living room.

Joanie was in deep analysis for two years before she met Bill, so she knows well the connection between her feelings for Emma and those she has now for Bill.

"I met Bill in an after-hours club, the Shandru, in Harlem that a black girl (blacks were the only ones I associated with at the time) knew. She introduced us and I guess we went for one another right away."

Bill told Joanie she was not doing anything much at the moment. A few jobs if you wanted to call them that, like, well, dealing here and there, working for a heroin pusher occasionally, working for a bookie now and then, gambling some. A bookkeeper by trade, she said she could earn more this way. There was not enough in straight work to pay for the way she liked to live. And she preferred to sleep during the day, anyway, and go out at night when she did most of her business. She lived alone.

In exchange for this information, Joanie told Bill about her parents, her lonely life without girl or boy friends. She told her how, except for the hours when she was in school, she spent most of her time alone in her room. In no time at all it was closing time at the Shandru. With no need for words, they headed for Bill's apartment.

"Go down to the basement and let yourself in while I pick up a couple of things for breakfast," Bill said, handing her the key.

Bill's room was a terrible place, sparsely furnished and grubby; Joanie felt miserable just to think of her living here.

On her return, Joanie remembers, Bill made coffee and cooked scrambled eggs on the two-burner stove and brought them to her. After eating, they fell into bed, exhausted.

"You're freezing, Joanie. Come here to me."

Bill's hands reached out and without hesitation Joanie went to her.

Although Joanie's loneliness had been so overpowering that often it had been nearly impossible to bear, only then, waking beside Bill, did she realize how bad it had been. Looking back across the empty hours before that night, she was amazed that she managed to get through them at all, that she managed to survive without the friendship of one single person, without the comfort of receiving or giving any love.

Not until Bill, a stranger, had she ever found someone to feel close to. She was full of gratitude, wanted desperately to do something for her—but Bill might not want her though. Bill had indicated she didn't mind her lonely life, that she got on well by herself. And what had Joanie to give her in return for the priceless gift of love and friendship? At last fully understanding the extent of her loneliness, she could not bear to think of returning to it.

Looking around the grubby, sordid room, she remembers thinking how good it would be if she and Bill could take a nice light apartment. How much easier it would be if Bill had someone to clean up for her, wash her clothes instead of having to do it for herself.

Suddenly, startling her, Bill echoed Joanie's thoughts.

"It's a pretty creepy pad, isn't it? I'm sorry I had to bring you here, but it's the best I can do. I'm in a little bit of trouble right now."

Joanie says she seized on the word. "Trouble? What kind of trouble? Can I help you out?"

Bill was quiet for a moment, then laughed and pulled Joanie down against her shoulder. "No, baby. You can't do anything. And anyway, why should you?"

Joanie repeated her offer. "If it's money, I'm sure I can help you."

Bill spoke to Joanie as if she were a child. She didn't know her: why should she offer her money? It could be a loan then if Bill preferred to think of it that way, said Joanie—and finally Bill agreed. If Joanie really, really meant it, it would be a big favor; she wouldn't pretend she couldn't do with a helping hand.

"I might as well tell you the truth," she said. "There's this guy I sometimes push horse for. The thing is I owe him two grand and he's not the type that's satisfied to wait. So I was going to leave town. But I don't want to . . . not now."

89

In a rush, Joanie's fear vanished: she knew *she* was the reason Bill didn't want to leave.

Later the two girls caught a cab to the bank where Joanie's money was deposited. Afterward, they ate lunch in a fancy restaurant, laughing like children at the people who stared at them with curiosity. Joanie never believed she could be so happy. Joanie and Bill continued their relationship, Joanie confident that no matter how much time she spent away from home nobody knew—or would care—about them. And then, suddenly, she discovered her parents knew every detail; they had seen her with Bill and put a private detective on their trail.

"Are you going to give that nigger up?" Joanie's father demanded.

Defiantly, she refused.

"In that case," he said coldly, "I don't want you in this house."

Which is how Joanie and Bill got to San Francisco.

Anise's story is not too different from Joanie's. While not rich like Joanie's, her parents are comfortably middle-class. And like Joanie, she had left home after a fight with her father who had objected to the last of her many affairs. After having known many men, "all of whom wanted to sleep with me, period, because they knew I'd be no great shakes as a wife, I met this man, Bob Green." Bob was completely different from Anise and her parents in income and education. Rough-spoken, with little schooling, he had worked many years as a merchant seaman. Already, at thirty-two, he had been twice divorced and was the father of three children he saw occasionally. Still, he needed Anise as much as she needed him. Neither had any notion of how temporary the need was.

Bursting with enthusiasm at having so much confusion in common (and in truth their problems often seemed identical) and eager to return to the fold, "the first thing I had us do together was to visit our families and tell them the good news. His family approved of me because they approved of my background, and my parents overlooked his crudity and gave us their blessing."

During the three months before her marriage, and rejoining conventional society, the penitent rebel had "dreams of 'His' and 'Hers' on both towels, of tiny feet and a cottage made for two." Smiling bitterly at the recollection, Anise says that for a year after they married, they continued to be good citizens and unbearably ordinary. Anise's parents, of course, were delighted with her, and embraced "the children" into the bosom of the family, where they nestled with increasing discomfort which neither would admit. Between them the discomfort grew, at first heavily masked with overanxious solicitude toward each other, later expressed more openly. They could hardly wait for the marriage to break up. But Anise knew she couldn't take the first step. "Bob walked off, finally, and really, I'd wanted to be sad as any ordinary woman would be. But I couldn't seem to make it. I felt relieved. We'd contracted many debts during our marriage, and my parents said that if we couldn't locate Bob, they'd help me pay them off. I said to forget the whole deal and I'd go back to San Francisco.

"My father loves me but he loves my mother more. He said, 'So you're going back to the way you used to live. Well, you're grown and can do as you want. I hope that someday you'll remember what you did to your mother.' He was pained, of course. But my father's pain is anger locked in ice.

"So here I came to S.F. and got a job in the crummy Blue Boat in North Beach. Well, you know what it's like—the atmosphere and all. Just plain dirty, and, in its way, criminal."

Narcotics are pushed in the Blue Boat, usually "soft stuff," marijuana and pills, but you can also score for heroin and LSD.

The stage is a small clearing surrounded by tables. A five-piece band of African-looking men, incongruously dressed in white knee-length beach pants, glowing purplish in the light, red loose-sleeved blouses tied at the stomach and beach hats with lurid dyed feathers, pounds cannibalistic music that tears at the senses, African-drumming, jungle-moaning. And Anise dances. Her almost nude body gleaming, lips purposely parted and teeth gnashing, she twists and grinds. In rhythmic, savagely convulsed movements, accompanied by proper guttural groans and facial expression, she simulates a woman's orgasm and ends by falling to the floor in a sweating, panting heap. Then rising, still writhing, she slithers to the band, takes the beach hat off the drummer's head and passes it among the crowd, commenting as she collects her money: "Enjoy your slumming tour, sister," to a well-dressed woman, and "How are you to-night, miss?" to an effeminate man. And withdrawing her hat abruptly from one of the male hustlers: "I'll take it out later in trade, honey."

"So you see, I'm nobody to be high and mighty about playing in Mann's movies." Then she says: "Here's something you'd be ashamed if you were writing fiction to put in your book. But it really happened." And she tells me how she was streetwalking during one of the times when her more legitimate resources were exhausted— one of those times when there was no work as a dancer and no films to be made.

It was a cold, rainy, bone-chilling San Francisco night when all at once she was conscious of a warning shiver of trouble. Every prostitute knows this premonition. "And you ought to act on what you know," Anise says. "My God, you ought to act on it."

Yet she swung around obediently at the male call "like a well-trained sea lion." For a moment she stared unbelievingly, her mind refusing to accept the identity of the man who called her.

It was her uncle.

"Anise. What are you doing here?"

"I couldn't sleep. I always try to walk myself to sleep when I can't."

"That's not true."

"Are you calling me a liar?" She was desperate.

"How long have you been doing this?" Anise's uncle

93

has the same rigid self-control as her father and she felt forced to answer him truthfully.

"I don't know, I really don't. Since I left home, I guess."

"You're coming home with me, right now."

"No."

Anise's uncle's face was stone-cast but so was hers. In the end, as both he and she knew he would, he walked off and left her—his admission that she was right: there *was* no way out for her.

Anise finishes her story in the monotonous tone she has employed throughout. Her eyes have reflected deep anguish; then, as if a switch were flicked, they become detached and expressionless. "Well," she says. "Period. Exclamation point."

Some San Francisco police authorities say that hard-core producers "just can't be caught. They're a slippery bunch, you know."

Mann laughs at that notion. "Oh, they know us all right. Me, for instance, they know to the tune of two grand or so whenever I make a new picture. And more than that if they want to bring in one of my kids because the censors are cracking down or something. When the censors start hollering, they've *got* to do something. They leave us producers alone—why not, with all the dough we shell out. But they'll pick up a couple of kids in the picture, say Joan or Anise or preferably the male hustlers, and they give them the business like, 'Who made that dirty film you played in and how can we get our hands on them?'

"Most kids won't tell, naturally. I mean, they wouldn't tell even if they weren't aware that the vice cops know our names and residences. The cops don't want the kids to tell, because, hell, if they did, then they'd have to do something about us and that wouldn't be to their advantage. So, instead, they publicize the *kids,* use them to tell John Q. Public: 'See, you can't blame us; it's these damn Tenderloin kids, those junkies who won't give us their names just like they won't help us catch the junk pushers even though they can finger them in a minute, and we can't do a thing without them.' The truth is, hard as it is on Joanie and Anise and Gene to make a movie like you've seen them do, you can go to any art film, even the mildest, those approved by the Supreme Court, and become far more erotically aroused than you'd be by the worst underground flicks. . . ."

V

The Customers: "They're So Ugly"

WHO are the customers for Mann's underground films? The moment I asked to be introduced to them, producers who had previously relished our conversations seemed suddenly full of indirection and subterfuge. Banded together, as they seldom were otherwise, they cat-padded every answer concerning even irregular customers, to say nothing of steady ones—and no wonder, in view of their lucrative business.

Only Mann, seemingly possessed with the need to prove that, despite Joanie and Anise and Gene, Luv and the Gorilla and Lee Lynch, his films have a valid reason for being, agreed to introduce me to two regular customers—a call-house madam and an avowed sadist, "speaking from their own personal experience, mind you. They'll tell you what my pictures mean to them; the help they get from every new one I put out."

The call-girl madam, Rita James, came to Mann's apartment to discuss her use of his movies. She was a tall relaxed blonde with a bored expression. She wore no makeup, but had on a pair of silver hoop earrings and although it was daytime was dressed entirely in silver—silver lamé sweater, skintight silver skirt, broad silver belt, silver Capezio slippers. Except for the lack of makeup she looked as if she had just stepped off some chorus line.

She said in a tone to match her bored expression, that for her, in the particular wilderness she must live in, pornographic pictures and movies are life-savers. She explained that her house is unlike most in San Francisco or elsewhere. In most houses, customers all want the same things from their girls. The same small talk, the same phrases, the same slight variations, "and you've got it made if you're an ordinary pro with ordinary tricks."

But Rita's house caters to a different kind of trick altogether. He is three things the ordinary customer is not—rich, a man with time on his hands, and almost always an urge to experience unusual sex. Unusual sex is what Rita's house is known for.

How, specifically, are Rita's tricks different from most? Well, take a little man who came some three weeks ago and still comes weekly. The first time he and Rita met, he told her he wanted to be with her rather than any of the girls. He would pay her two hundred dollars for two hours of her time. But he didn't want to go to her house to see her; instead, he wanted her to come to his hotel penthouse suite. When she arrived there, he led her into the apartment, shut the door behind her and turned the key. Then he poured drinks.

"Hurry up and get undressed now," he ordered without preliminaries. Something in his voice frightened Rita. She took her dress off and when she turned to face him in her slip, she became aware of a strange wild look in his eyes.

"Get undressed, I said."

She hesitated for a moment and he came toward her with upraised fists.

"Come here."

She went toward him, trying to smile though knowing from past experience what would happen. And it did. He beat, punched and kicked her. Then, fully dressed as he had been since she arrived, he gave her the two hundred dollars, told her to get dressed and unlocked the door so that she was free to go.

"Well, he came back and I took him on again because I needed the money. Only this time, I insisted he come to my house and let me show him some of Mann's films before he began on me. I hoped he might get his kicks out of the films and then some of the pressure'd be off me. I turned out to be right too. He watched the pictures and jerked off. He still hit me some but nothing like he'd done the first time."

Rita sat hunched forward, the pulse in her throat beating visibly. "I really think the picture had its effect. I've seen it happen more than once with sadistic customers. They calm down, not always, of course, but often enough so I can recommend them to other girls in my business who get men as mean as this one."

Mann says Rita is not his only call-girl customer.

Others, hardly newcomers to their business, have their fair share of sadistic customers, and they, too, subscribe to Rita's statement. He names girls who explain the effectiveness of the films in diminishing the men's drives, in much the same terms, interestingly, as analysts and therapists who have similar patients.

"The way it seems to work with this trick I told you about and some others like him I go with now and then because the money's such a hell of a lot better than ordinary tricks would pay," Rita says, "is that he sees himself as the man in the picture who's doing the beating. It's an outlet for him so he doesn't have to take everything in him out on me. He can slow up once we get going, you know.

"There was one nut who masturbated while the movie was on and then paid me my money though he didn't even lay a finger on me. I didn't lose him either. In fact, he's one of my most faithful tricks. It seems the movie alone isn't enough to satisfy him. He needs me in the room with him while he watches and masturbates. Just the movie going and me there, maybe holding his hand or just sitting doing nothing's enough to relieve him."

Fritz Bober, a wealthy industrialist, is, like Rita, one of Mann's staunchest supporters.

"And Fritz," Mann says, "is a sadist himself."

Fritz is a handsome, stocky man of fifty or so with a lusty laugh and a long series of Rabelaisian jokes he throws off one after the other. He is obviously cultivated and well-educated. His living room is tastefully furnished and lined with books, many of them first editions. Unlike other wealthy men of his acquaintance, he buys them for his own personal pleasure, not as investments.

Comfortably seated in his scarlet satin-covered easy chair with coffee cup and cigarette, Fritz Bober proved to have an insatiable lust for self-revelation that must sometimes prove vastly humiliating. Disclosing his private sexual woes, his conversation was so loaded with pain at his description of himself as a sadist that it became almost unbearable to listen to. He told, with terrible contempt and self-hatred, every minute detail of his fantasies about hurting women—flagellating them, tying them up, making incisions in their flesh and pouring hot wax in the wounds.

"And there was a time," he said, "when I went to prostitutes and carried my desires into practice, but the shame afterward was too great.

"Once I hurt a girl so badly she had to be hospitalized. And once, not knowing what I was doing, I almost killed a streetwalker I'd picked up and brought back here. I was wretched, of course. I gave the girls money, but that didn't diminish my feeling of vileness.

"I've been under psychiatric care for years, but I never found any help on the couch. I've contemplated suicide many times because I'm so frightened of my instincts. And I tell myself I'd rather be dead than kill somebody else. But, somehow, I've never had the courage to follow through. I've also thought of committing myself to a mental hospital where I'd be unable to do the physical hurt I've done people in the past.

"Oh, I've paid those I've hurt, of course, and because money's no problem I've paid them so well that they've been willing to accept all kinds of indignities. Poor girls, most of them have a touch of masochism in them anyway. And the ones with demanding pimps will do anything for money. But, actually, when you've subjected any human being to what I've put some of those girls through, you feel that there isn't enough money in the world to pay them off."

Fritz Bober said he has not had to go to prostitutes so often since he discovered Mann's sado-masochistic pictures, all of which he has bought for his collection. "In a sense," he said thoughtfully, "I've fantasied while watching them, and by dint of that have been able, so far, to divorce my desires from actual acts. Not that Mann's films have dammed up my instinctual drives— they're mighty feelings, and I've found nothing to stop them. But the pictures, coupled with a fear of consequence over any overt act I might commit, keep me from doing what I used to. They're an outlet, a substitute satisfaction that's holding me, for the time being anyhow, from exploding. I haven't hurt anyone for some time now."

Some authorities, including America's chief of law enforcement, J. Edgar Hoover, a man certainly experienced in dealing with sexual psychopaths, is in thorough disagreement with Rita and Fritz Bober.

"We know," he has stated, "that in an overwhelmingly large number of cases, sex crime is associated with pornography . . . movies, books, etc. I believe pornography is a major cause of sex violence."

Mr. Hoover's view has been endorsed by many law enforcement officers and also a number of cognitive witnesses who testified to that effect before a Congressional committee on proscribing the circulation of obscene and pornographic materials. Inspector Harry Fox of the Philadelphia Police Department, for example, presented many actual case studies of adult and juvenile criminals in his jurisdiction who had possessed large collections of such matter, including hard-core pornographic movies.

On the other hand, renowned sexologists Drs. Phyllis and Eberhard Kronhausen say, in their definitive book *Pornography and the Law,* that hard-core pornography (including portrayals of sadistic acts) "may be more often than not a safety valve for the sexual deviate . . . catharsis through vicarious participation."

As one illustration of their oft-repeated premise, they offer this case-study of a patient they label E. whom Dr. Eberhard Kronhausen treated for many years. In his middle twenties when he came to Dr. Kronhausen, he had never succeeded in consummating a sexual relation with a girl. Every time he tried to do so, he suffered from a premature ejaculation.

"This patient's masturbation fantasies consisted mainly

of scenes of human sacrifice, of monsters making off with helpless female victims, of himself as a vampire, attacking a woman, sinking his claws into her, ripping her body open.

"And yet he was capable of holding a fairly responsible job, of doing voluntary community work in his spare time and of generally keeping in remarkably good touch with reality."

"Here was an example of sadistic imagery almost fully supplanting natural erotic impulses. Several times," the Kronhausens report, "the patient brought in certain horror magazines which excited him tremendously, only to be distressed to discover that the therapist was not excited by them. When the therapist, in turn, brought in a series of girlie magazines they produced no response—except for one girlie magazine which contained pictures of a fully dressed female whose facial expressions seemed to indicate she was being tortured and in great pain.

"Once he made a valiant effort to reform by destroying his entire collection of pictures and weapons, but became so restless and disturbed that therapist feared really serious consequences. It was, therefore, a relief for patient and therapist alike when patient announced he could not fight his evil nature longer and had made a start of a new collection. Immediately, he became quieter and able to function more effectively in other areas of his life, which were relatively unaffected by his sexual problem."

The Kronhausens conclude:

"We believe that it is (clinically) very dangerous to

block by critical or prohibitory attitudes and activities the few remaining fantasy outlets of sexually disturbed individuals."

One cannot help but wonder, as the Kronhausens do, what would have happened if the patient, instead of making the adjustment he did in his community, had gone out and murdered or raped. They say, in answer to their supposition, "the weapons and the pornography would doubtless be played up—that he had them in his possession. This has always been the case in such murder cases. It is always easier and socially more comfortable to blame a person's reading or pornographic movie viewing for a hideous crime than to explore and expose the poisoned family and societal dynamics which are more closely related to the crime, delving more deeply into the social and personal causes."

Both the noted sexologist Dr. Wardell Pomeroy and Dr. Benjamin Karpman, chief psychotherapist of Saint Elizabeth's Hospital in Washington, D.C., concur with the Kronhausens.

Many pornographic films and photographs are, of course, not sadistic. Jean Morgan, niece of an important pornographer and photographer in New York who specializes in such fare, is her uncle's prime distributor and solicitor for actors and actresses. Jean, twenty-nine, dark-haired and pretty, is more relaxed than many of her male cohorts, but, strangely, seems less soft than they. She believes this to be "natural," claiming that there is no place in her world for "weak sisters." In the world in which she was born and raised and in which she moves presently—a man's world—feminine softness can only lead to getting hurt by men, invite trickery, open the door for the profiteer retailer on the one hand and the vice-squad officer on the take on the other. To be a successful pornographer Jean says you must be, or at least pretend to be, invulnerable. Especially if you're a woman.

We met the first time in her favorite jazz club with its bar and small band in New York's East Fifties. After that we went to the Greenwich Village clubs where Jean recruits most of her uncle's models and actresses.

"Well, you know how it is, the dancers in these clubs can't last there forever and when the time comes for them to leave, they ask around here and there, 'Do you know a job I can get for a while that isn't hustling?' So here I am, Johnny-on-the-spot, with an offer for them to pose. Of course, we don't pay as much as California. We only pay twenty-five dollars for a series of straight nude portraits which we transfer to playing cards and either distribute through the prostitutes and nightclub dancers on our list for three dollars a deck or sell for ten to twenty-five dollars a pack at conventions and stag parties where we exhibit our movies. And we do make porny movies which, if our clients weren't such jerks, they'd never buy in a million years. I mean, they're nothing, really."

She pulled a file out of her purse and began to work at a fingernail while she talked of her and her uncle's customers, very different from Mann's. "They're primarily squares, you know. And their dames go along with them because what else can they do, after all? I mean, women are women but they're married to men . . ."

Actually, Jean said, you see comparatively few worldly-wise wives at men's "stags"; even those married to organization men whom they've accompanied to their conventions. The men, of course, are excellent customers for pornographic films. Most don't have to pay a fee to see them. One of Jean's best agents, "a gray-flannel type himself, invites them, after the less exclusive parties and meetings in the large hotel dining rooms to small intimate rooms where, after they've been properly sated with whiskey, they stretch out on wide couches and comfortable chairs and watch the pictures.

"They're the worst of any I know, and maybe that's why you wouldn't catch them bringing their wives along. Or maybe the wives are too independent to come. But those so-called respectable men's reactions, ugh. They're so—well—ugly, really."

She described at length the jaunty executive sophisticates, to whom these movies are "old hat," just one more way of relaxing after work, and the many unsophisticated who are quite clearly thrilled by what they are seeing.

"They, unlike union men and Elk and Mason members, leave women out of the parties. Being by themselves, they can really let themselves go. I'm there, sure, but I don't count as a woman in their minds. I'm like another man to them. They just talk in front of me any way they feel. Their language isn't controlled either. I've never heard such words from truck drivers as I have from these pillars of the community." She laughed. "These good family men with all their good, old-fashioned virtues. I mean, men who look like butter wouldn't melt in their mouths talking so even I find myself blushing. And you'd better believe I'm not an easy blusher."

Jean said that stag and business parties don't necessarily end when the movies are done. "The men know— I tell them—that the performers they've seen in my films are available to them at a fee, usually a hefty one. Ordinary stags can't afford the girls; the men who can don't have to, actually. They're usually staked by the businesses who intend to get something in return for that little service."

It is the wealthy and most successful men—members of the most exclusive clubs, not only in New York, Chicago, Houston, Los Angeles and the other large cities but also in the smaller ones, like Dubuque, Kansas City and Wilmington, Delaware—who rent and sometimes purchase pornographic films and also command from the producers' contact men "introductions" to pornographic players in whom they become interested. They pay one hundred dollars and up to meet the girls. The price, of course, depends on many things; the kind of relations they expect to have with a girl, the length of time they want with her, and her—and their—home bases. Some fly a girl to their hometown, paying all her expenses. It is not unusual among these men for two or three to share in paying her fees and expenses and to mutually use her services.

However, most viewers, especially from smaller towns where they run a chance of discovery by family, friends and associates, prefer no truck with a "porny-actress prostitute." Would-be tricks from smaller cities, therefore, either meet the girls where they live or someplace between.

Jean's regular film purchasers, with the exception of the deviates, rent them wherever they have contacts— to stag parties and country clubs, for example. Her purchasers of films include a former insurance salesman who figured shrewdly that he could earn more money by giving up his business and concentrating on planning the extracurricular activities of his former colleagues during insurance conventions from coast to coast, a dress manufacturer's son who has contacts with women's wear manufacturers, and a former tennis club champion and country club president in one of the wealthier suburbs of New York.

"For him, as for everyone in underground pornies," Jean said, "the country club business is tops. Because most country-clubbers, being on the wealthy side, wouldn't have trouble with the vice-men no matter what they did. Unlike the smaller fish who are prime targets for pickups."

Vice-men in the larger cities, talking off the record, say Jean is absolutely right. The kindly and compassionate lieutenant in charge of the sixteen-man morals squad of a medium-sized Midwest city genially said that he and his men were aware of the regular showing of pornographic movies at one of the most exclusive country clubs in his city.

They were delivered to the club's social director by mail. The legal department of the U.S. post office almost always prosecutes both the sender and the knowing recipient of "obscene material" sent through the mails. And local police and morals-squad men confiscate obscene material and prosecute anyone who possesses such material if they believe it was intended for sale, rather than for the individual's use. Yet they prosecute neither the country-clubbers nor their salesman—ever.

"We here know for a fact that after this exclusive club has its fill of the obscenity it buys at first hand and for a fancy fee, one to three thousand dollars, it sells it to other clubs," the vice-man says. "Now, since we on our squad know that this club's obscene movies arrive by mail, you can't tell me the post office people don't know too. How come, then, they don't prosecute? And, by the same token, how come we don't?

"I'll tell you how come; the club members aren't just loaded, they're among our most highly respected citizens. Friends not only of the judges but also of the mayor and governor. That's why we have to keep our eyes closed or at least our mouths shut. But what about the post office department? Why don't they do something? Well, the answer to that one's not so tough either. I also happen to know that some of the members have an in with certain big shots in Washington.

'So, OK, those showings are private. The obscene movies, they're shown in a private club where my kids or I couldn't see them if we wanted to. So the way I feel is that what people show, in private, to their own consenting membership is the membership's business, not mine or the post office's or the President's of the United States for that matter. But what does bug me is this: if these same underground films were sent to a poor men's club, *also private,* you can bet your bottom dollar the Federal post-office fellows would discover them, and—oh boy! There'd be a nice trial with newspaper coverage and all, making local heroes out of the Federal post-office lawyers, our own D.A., yours truly, my morals-squadders and everybody else as examples of the way we uphold the morality laws.

"The same goes for wife-swappers as country club members. Actually, many wife-swappers *are* country club members. People don't know that. They don't know the number of wife-swappers either, not only in big cities but also in those the size of ours. It's phenomenal. What would you think, for instance, if I told you that if my superiors really wanted to raid all the swappers whose names I know—forget those I don't—I could keep four of my sixteen-man squad busy full time!

"Talk of your hypocrisy! In the entire history of wife-swapping in this country, there has been only one swapping group uncovered. Only one. And the members of that one were post-office patsies during a time when the obscenity squad was under criticism and the department *had* to do something about the mailing of pornographic movies. There was a hell of a lot of pressure on them. And without knowing it they found that some of the producers of that underground film-making they'd decided to go after were also swappers.

"Well, naturally. Many swappers, though not all by a long shot, are exhibitionists. They like to have themselves photographed in exotic sex positions. And they like to show themselves off to other swappers who'll appreciate them, so they order films like mad. So all you've got to do to get the swappers is to get your hands on the underground mail films. No big deal. But, hell, we're not about to do it; why get involved with swappers and their important contacts when you can get just as much credit if you're a vicer like me by picking on the people everyone else picks on—the pros, the homos, the hustlers?"

The lieutenant, rare for a vicer, pauses for quite a long time. Finally he tells me that he doesn't want to be misunderstood. He doesn't think, personally, that swappers, pornographic viewers or producers or any other people who find their sexual satisfactions in ways other than the rest of us should be punished for following their own sexual bents.

"Look," he says, "if I'm entitled to my kind of sex for me, they are to theirs too. Because—well, really, I don't think that because I live the same sex life most people do, I've any right to condemn those who are different. They've got their reasons for doing what they do, the way I look at it."

VI

"Pretend to Be My Wife...
Wear Something Homey"

JOHN M. LAWRENCE (for reasons that will soon be apparent, this is not his real name) is director of the crime commission of a large, crime-infested city. In his early forties, he is, on the surface, a highly moral man, father of six children, a pious and habitual churchgoer.

I first met John Lawrence at a meeting of policemen and vice-squadders, judges, district attorneys, and members of the local Citizens for Decent Literature. "We're lucky," he says in a voice of camaraderie, "to have our able C.D.L. national expert among us today, knowing how full our town is of smut, of dirt that corrupts our children daily and humiliates us every time we walk into a drugstore."

He plays to the men, not the women. He is *masculine!* "Come on, fellows," he urges them. "Let's get the ball rolling. Let's do our best to make this filthy city fit for our kids. Let's make it a place where they can walk the streets without having dirt thrown at them."

After numerous questions have been asked and answered, teams are organized to go on a shopping tour of restaurants and candy stores for pornographic materials John knows can be bought over the counter.

The teams return bringing magazines, a few paper-cover books with lurid covers, and a set of still photos of near-nude women in erotic poses—surely, nothing that this audience, long accustomed to haunting pornographic bookshops, hasn't seen hundreds of times before. But under John's guidance the audience acts shocked, the women awed by the evidence of "smut." John Lawrence has won more supporters for a new and larger "anti-smut campaign to give our kids the best present in the world—a clean, wholesome city in which to grow up."

After the meeting he and I go to dinner, in the course of which I ask him questions about his city, and the subject of wife-swapping comes up. He exhibits great interest. He has a collection of materials on the subject and offers to share it with me if I come to his office.

It seems strange to me that the crime investigating commission of a city like this, riddled with gangsterism, murderers, and narcotics dealers, should be investigating so basically limited an area. But he doesn't find it strange at all. He laughs softly. "Well, the reason we're investigating wife-swappers is that we want to know if there's blackmail involved. Is there fraud involved? Do people take pornographic photos of other people in the club and then say, 'Give me so much money or I'll send these pictures to your children'? Or 'I'll send them to your family. Or to the newspapers.' We're really working to save the innocent swappers who must be protected from the ones who would use them."

He then says that, if I wish, he'll not only offer me tutelage but a passport into a club so that I can learn for myself what goes on.

"Now, keep in mind," he says with an indulgent smile, "I'd never do anything to embarrass you. All there'd be is talk between you and me, pretending to be husband and wife, and another couple. We'd have what's—you know—a preliminary interview. Never follow through, of course. But you learn plenty in those preliminary interviews. There are two other women I work with now—you know, pretending to be my wife. What I do, when I'm working with these other two, I advertise in these bulletins, these wife-swapping bulletins, you know. And I write as the wife, saying we're fun-loving, with exotic tastes and interested in meeting other fun-loving couples, attractive, and with the same tastes as ours. Then, from there, we see where we go.

"Come to think of it, I've got a woman coming in on Wednesday to talk about a swap-party between my 'wife' and myself and her husband and her. They're both college graduates. But she doesn't want to talk to me alone. Although she makes all the decisions for her and her husband, she's got to make sure the wife'll appeal to him. So she doesn't want to see me alone. So this could be fun. We could pretend to be husband and wife. Together we could put over a good one. Do you think you can? As I've said, it'll only be talk. I'll see to it. And I'd cue you in

on what to say when you meet this woman. Because our
stories, you know, would have to jibe."

I decide to string him along for the moment. "Tell
me, John, what would I wear on an appointment working with you?"

"You could get away with wearing just about anything you wanted to. Something glamorous or something simple and homey or—you know. Some of these
gals," he says in confidence, "some of these gals I've run
across, have kind of accentuated the few charms they did
have. There's one gal had a dress on that was so tight I
still have to smile about it. She could hardly walk.
Honestly."

I laugh over the woman in the tight dress and again
ask him what I would wear. "I think it ought to be something homey. After all, if I'm supposed to be in my own
home . . ."

"Yes. Well, I think that would be natural. But whatever you'd wear would be great. But, you know, they
really don't care what you do wear. All they're interested in is the sex—such a boring bunch of people. [My
own researches proved just the opposite.] Nobody asks
much or wants to know much about you. The only thing
you have to be careful about is not to have anyone involved who is not able to pull off a good act. Because it
could be dangerous in this respect. If you ran across a
badgering team which didn't trust you, you'd never
know what could happen."

"Yes, that's what I was going to ask you. What *could*
happen?"

"Well, if you and I made them think we were investigating them, there's no telling what they'd do. But all I'd have to do is to tell you a little bit more—"

"Would I act naïve, or what?"

"Well, what I do with the other ones I use, I tell them not to talk too much. Then I explain to the others that they're a little shy when it comes to conversation but they make up for it in other ways. This always seems to go across because I guess just about everybody goes for a person who isn't mouthing it up all the time. On the female end, I mean. This way's always worked well.

"And if anyone asks too much about you, which they won't do, usually because all they care about's appearance and whether you'd be interested in their kind of sex, we just say you'd rather not go into your background too much. It's one you have to guard a little carefully. There are people with whom you're working who would sort of frown on this type of activity. In fact, we don't even tell our last names. And, actually, we're interested in other things, not your background. We like what we see and hope they feel the same."

"Yes, but when we first meet a swapping couple, what would be my relationship to the woman I mean, would we engage in woman talk or something?"

"No," he says, "everything's sexually oriented. If you're not talking directly about the type of sex we're going to have—directly—you're talking about the wonderful couple that we ran across the last time we had a party. You might mention that she has an interesting job—she's with some designer and is always running back and forth to Paris. She introduced us to the Parisian night life—you know, things of this sort."

He changes the subject abruptly. "Let me ask you this. Would it be possible for you to get over one day—so I could really show you around the place. I think I have one of the most unique setups you've ever seen."

"Well, I'm supposed to be a hostess . . ."

"Sure, a hostess has to know where the booze is, right?"

He tells me now, buoyantly and with complete assurance I'll do as he wishes, that there's got to be one stipulation. "This has got to be ultra-confidential, between you and me. When I say confidential, I mean that I don't talk to my wife about this, and this is something your husband couldn't be put wise to."

I hesitate a moment as though unsure of being able to follow through on this aspect.

"It would be a great experience for you. Really, I mean it. You'll be glad you came, because let me tell you, we'll have a game there the likes of which neither one of us will ever get into again. . . ."

VII

Before We Began to Swing

AN AMIABLE, young, well-bred face, a mouth smiling with a gamin wistfulness, and a very low drawl. Certainly there's nothing sinister about this Adele McLean, who had been chosen, out of the eight members of a Westchester wife-swappers' club, to give structure and sequence to what was to me, on the day I met her, a jumble of facts and impressions stored in my mind. Surely swappers couldn't participate in such weird rites; they couldn't openly confess their doings, making such statements as: "My wife's an angel in her fashion—and I'm not being ironic when I say 'fashion'—but" or: "It's meant so much to me being married to my husband. Being his wife's been the loveliest thing in my life. I love him, I really do, he's my favorite person in the world. But, you see, our marriage—"

I had been steered to Adele's swap club by Jean (swappers are some of her best customers) and by the Midwest vice lieutenant. I had met Adele in a midtown restaurant. She had said at the beginning of our meeting,

"Really, I'm not very knowledgeable about swinging. Paul and I are fairly new members of the swingers." She sounded as if she envied the older clubbers' full life before she and her husband had also become swingers or "modern marrieds," as the wife-swappers throughout the country, from Los Angeles to Boston and Denver to Miami, identify themselves to each other.

As Adele bent very low to talk to me, I felt like a predator as I fingered my long list of pious, disrespectful questions—a list headed by that fatuous question: "Tell me about it. Why do you do it?"

This, of course, is what four out of every five interviewers have always asked the female—especially fastidious female—swap-club members. What a futile question! It is the same question that is thrown at prostitutes, and it deserves the same answer they provide whenever their customers put the query—the first thing that comes to mind in hopes of politely blocking more presumptuous queries. Why shouldn't they be on the defensive before the lynxlike curiosity of men, who, though they use them in private, have been educated to "spit" on them in public?

Similarly, why should a wife-swapper surrender her caution and wariness to people who not only may identify her but cause her to be condemned by the upright, respected citizens who accept her because they know nothing of her swapping activities?

Some women wife-swappers, of course, are not defensive at all; indeed, they blatantly let you know that their life adjustment is better than yours. They tell you, because they believe it, that unlike you, who out of cowardice are saddled with mental and physical frustrations, they have found the way, the only way (for to them sex is the only way) of facing life honestly.

Fully convinced that, although you may not altogether grasp their meaning, you nevertheless must covet their liberation, they do not hesitate to lay bare the most intimate secrets of their lives with their husbands and swap-partners. For the true believers in "modern-marriedism," no detail of their sexuality is too personal; not, at least, once they have come to know you and to trust your promise to protect their anonymity. And the higher up they are in their social circles, the more pride they take in their activities.

Anita Lewis is a mini-skirted ingenue wife of a Chicago lawyer, who, although she is a psychiatric social worker, looks like a musical-comedy star. She blows the most impeccable smoke rings, flicking ashes from her constantly lit cigarette with excessive daintiness as she throws out confidences that would startle debonair women twice her age: "I haven't got sufficient words to describe the satisfaction, the stimulation, the delight in our own marriage as well as in our 'co-marital partnerships' my husband and I have experienced since we came to our understanding and began swinging."

Anita is like all consecrated "modern marrieds" I met individually or with their spouses or in groups as large as twenty, or with whom I corresponded by mail. She sharply distinguishes "co-marital" exchanges of two or more husbands and their wives from "extramarital" affairs, which she considers "disreputable."

Marlena Anderson, a forty-three-year-old grandmother living in Washington, D.C., and married to a man of more than middling importance in governmental circles, echoes young Anita. Marlena, who practically pushes on friends and acquaintances pictures of her two young grandchildren, invariably wears brave, large hats and black dresses specially cut to attract men's stares to her bare, white shoulders and voluptuous breasts. One dress and tricorne hat in particular makes her look like nothing so much as the cover illustration for the book *In Praise of Older Women by a Young Man.*

Once she let herself go with me—it took a long time—Marlena talked far more recklessly and freely than Anita about her marriage in relation to her "co-marital" sensations and emotions, experiments and experiences.

"My feelings about my husband," she said, "used to be, especially as we both grew older, equally divided between love and hate. I loved him for his brilliant intellect, his genuineness, his kindliness, his love and passion for me which continued through twenty-five years of marriage. But I hated him because his aging body reminded me that I was aging too, although he kept flattering me whenever we made love, and it was often, because George is still today, at fifty-three, a very passionate man—disgustingly passionate, I thought before we became swingers; he literally nauseated me in bed in spite of my respect for him as a person. You see, he'd had an illness two years before we started to swing that turned him scrawny, made his complexion bad, caused his skin to turn slack and sag so I couldn't stand any sort of bodily contact with him.

"Of course, he was too perceptive not to realize how he revolted me physically, although I did my best to hide it from him, out of compassion, to say nothing of my love for him.

"Strange as it may seem, it was George who first suggested we become swingers. And, you know, though I was fully aware, naturally, that he was considering my needs rather than his own, I was deeply hurt. I felt snubbed, rejected. And I couldn't understand how such an idea could have occurred to a man of his intellect and status. I mean, all I knew about swinging then came from titles I'd only glimpsed on covers of cheap magazines I'd never dream of buying. It certainly didn't seem an answer for people like us.

"At first, I laughed, sure that George must be joking. Then, when I discovered how deadly serious he was, I flew into a fury and began raving and ranting at him. What did he think I was, anyhow—some dime-store clerk, some whore? Or maybe he thought I was oversexed. Well, *he* was the oversexed one. As far as I was concerned, I didn't care if I never went to bed with a man again. And I didn't mean George alone, either; I meant any man.

"The grandchildren weren't born then, but both my daughters were grown—Jean was nineteen and Lisa was twenty-two and engaged to be married. So you can see how ridiculous the whole notion seemed to me. But George had done a lot of soul searching himself before he broached the idea to me, and he just kept at it and at me, selling the merits of the whole swinging situation.

"And then, a couple of months after he and I had first begun talking about swinging we spent a long weekend at Rehoboth Beach with two very dear friends. Lou's a doctor and Anne's what I guess you'd call a perennial student. She's got her master's degree in psychology, her Ph.D. in sociology and she still goes to school. Also, she paints and is a wonderful pianist though she's never performed publicly, out of fear, I think, rather than because she isn't good enough.

"Lou's thirty-six and Anne's thirty-one. But the difference in our ages made no difference in our friendship. Washington is like that, different from every other place in the United States I've ever known in that age isn't half as important in your relationship with people as mutual interests. Our friends, I mean, good, close friends, range from couples in their twenties to some in their late sixties and early seventies.

"I guess I'm going about it the long way, but, what I mean to say is that the four of us swung that weekend at Rehoboth and are still swinging now (we get away together twice a month or thereabouts) without any thought of age difference."

Marlena admitted to being somewhat horrified at her first swapping experience. Too many of those recollections seemed—despite the delight she says she will treasure for the rest of her life—a "shattering tragedy."

There was scarcely a minute during the three nights she spent with Lou and Anne with George, "except, of course, when we made love and I forgot everything but Lou"—with his firm resilient body—that flashes of her daughters were not evoked. During the times Lou slept, Marlena lay tossing and sleepless beside him, thinking of Joan and Lisa. She could not help imagining how, with their conventional upbringing, much like her own, her daughters would have loathed the thought of their mother in the arms of a man other than their father. She fought those thoughts with every defense she had— to no avail. No matter how she tried to block her thoughts, she could visualize the inevitable scene—the girls furious, and herself attempting to appease them with lies and promises she knew she might or might not be able to keep.

She could think of only one way to end the nightmare dominating her: wake Lou and make love again. But how could she do such a thing? Although Marlena may appear a woman of sophistication, actually she is—or was —extremely reticent and modest as befits the daughter of resolute Baptist parents who taught her that the only kind of lovemaking any woman would engage in—even with the man she married—was what both Marlena and her husband now refer to as "conventional."

I spoke with George later on and he reiterated all Marlena had told me. He said that although he loved her now as he had from the day they were married, he had always been frustrated by her refusal to engage in any sort of foreplay to intercourse. Through twenty-five

years she clung to her feminine modesty, stubbornly refusing to yield to any of his needs for stimuli.

"I would have done anything to stimulate her," George
said. "Out of selfish as well as unselfish reasons, because I myself become far more excited and aroused when
I'm able to rouse her. But she insisted—before we began
to swing, I mean—that these 'unnatural games'—that's
what she called all sexual foreplay—had no place in love
between a woman and a man.

"She still has a beautiful body," he said. "But she'd
never allow me to see her nude in all the many years before we began swinging. Can you imagine? To have been
married to a woman for years and never to have been allowed to see her?

"I don't know, to this day, how or why I stood for it,
except that I loved her so much and kept on hoping something would happen to change her."

Marlena laughed when I told her, with his permission,
all George had told me. "It was a long wait, wasn't it?
And if not for the swinging it would have been longer
still. Poor George. But the swinging's changed me, not
only with Lou and Jim, who is part of the one other wonderful couple we swing with occasionally, but also George
when he and I are making love. And George is so delighted in the change in me." She told me that before
she had begun swinging, she felt herself forced to cling
to her "mother's and grandmother's customs. I wanted
to perform the act quietly buried beneath a blanket in
a dark, secluded bedroom." She laughed.

"But getting back to my first night with Lou—be-

cause, really, in its way, that's what changed all our lives
—I wakened him after I found myself so miserable over
the kids. Being who I was then, you can't imagine what
it cost me to do that."

She talked passionately as she described how, despite
her firm belief that a woman ought never to be the ag-
gressor, she kissed Lou awake with her searching mouth.

"I could not believe it was me behaving so wantonly."

What happened next, Marlena said, she will never
forget.

" 'I didn't want to waken you,' I told Lou, 'but I
need you, now.'

" 'I'm glad,' he said, and immediately removed my
nightgown and his pajamas and turned on the bed lamp,
something I'd never let George do in all the years of our
marriage. He literally pored over my body for half an
hour, and, though I was embarrassed, I wouldn't have
had him stop for anything in the world. And then he
caressed me all over."

When George had caressed her through her night-
clothes, she said, "even at the beginning of our marriage, I'd occasionally—but only occasionally—permit
him to turn on the light. But, far from being stimulated,
my whole mood for lovemaking would be spoiled. And
I don't believe it was because of George. I just felt his
embraces and especially his tongue kisses to be more
than I could take—especially in the light. I think that
before swinging freed me, I'd have felt the same no matter whom I'd been with."

Her first night with Lou, though, she was aroused as

she knew he was also to a state of intense excitement by the most thorough, unhampered preliminaries. And instead of keeping her eyes closed as she had all her life during the sexual act, she opened them wide and looked directly at Lou. Soon something that had never happened before and that she never could have envisaged happening occurred. She began exploring Lou's chest, arms, cheeks, neck, legs.

"Neither of us slept all night except on and off," she said, "and we both had several orgasms."

In the morning, the two couples met for breakfast in the hotel dining room. Covering her embarrassment with an attempt at acting bold, Marlena preceded Lou to the table where George and Anne were sitting, looking like two people who thoroughly knew and accepted each other. Coming upon them like that, Marlena was surprised at her shiver of jealousy; could George's night with Anne, young Anne, have been as heady and intoxicating as hers with Lou? She admits she was horrified at the prospect.

Seeing George so obviously delighted and betraying none of the inadequacy he did after she and he made love, she felt her own exhilaration give way to guilt again. She found herself shaking with rage at her husband, eating breakfast so calmly while all she felt like was crying over her daughters deceived by their faithless parents.

She waited for the tears to come, but they didn't. Instead, she turned to Lou and the heady, intoxicating feeling she had when she was in his arms returned. George smiled at her lovingly, his face full of devotion; and then Anne softly complimented her on George's technique as a lover, his tact and finesse. "He goes to such elaborate lengths to please a woman," she told Marlena.

Marlena didn't know what Anne meant "although, as I've said, I certainly know now," but she wouldn't admit it to Anne or any other living soul. Having seen another woman in relation to George, she suddenly realized that though Lou enraptured *her* (as George, of all people, seemed to have delighted Anne), her basic attachment was to her husband just as Anne's was to Lou.

"After breakfast," Marlena said, "the four of us went swimming and later we looked for a new restaurant— we're all gourmets and one of our real kicks is exploring new restaurants."

At lunch, over too many drinks, Lou and Anne told Marlena that they had engaged in swapping activities for over three years—beginning some four years after their marriage. They told dozens of stories, not only of their co-marital relationships but also of their different activities as members of swapping groups of six, eight and even ten people.

"I seem to have blocked out much of what then was, to me, their 'vulgarity,'" Marlena said. "They talked about the 'little erotic games' they and the larger groups they'd swung with played, so they could become animated, incited, call it what you will, to the swinging mood.

"I do remember, though, that George didn't seem embarrassed at Anne's and Lou's conversation." Marlena remembers sitting there, her hands flat on either side of her chair "to prevent myself from getting up and running away, I guess, and smiling down at my shoes and hoping nobody could read my thoughts. Then, suddenly, Anne asked, 'Are you listening, Marlena?'

" 'Yes,' I said, feeling goose bumps on my arms because I had really been thinking that it was one thing to go to bed in private with a man who attracted you, though even that was bad enough, God knows . . . but this . . . to consciously swap your husband for your friend's; it seemed fighting against everything human. We seemed animals instead of ordinary, maybe somewhat extraordinary people.

"I came up for air just in time to hear Anne explaining about games people played when they attended swap-parties. She talked of the 'underground movies' they'd show to make people hot. That was Anne's word, 'hot,' and you'd have to see her to imagine how really incongruous it sounded coming out of her mouth. She's so —well, delicate and refined. I was really shocked at her description of the 'movies to put you in the mood.' But I was most revolted by her explanation of the swap-party games. I was horrified at them.

"If you'd ask me now why that was, I don't believe I could tell you. Now that I swap myself, I mean." She glanced down at her long, tapered hands resting in her lap. "Oh, the games Anne explained weren't different from ordinary card games people play except that, when you lost, you gradually stripped off items of clothing. They were both single—like poker and blackjack—and double-handed, which I've since learned most swingers, especially accustomed ones, choose over singles. These included hearts, pinochle, canasta. In them, you see, husbands and wives are allied against other husbands and wives. The winners undress the losers; the winning husband undressing the losing wife and vice-versa until everybody's in the nude. Naturally, a great deal of touching, kissing and caressing goes on till everybody's sort of excited or, anyhow, stimulated.

"Then there are the kinds of games with variations. Children's party games with variations. Remember Musical Chairs you played when you were a kid? Well, some swingers play Musical Laps. When the music begins, the women standing on the inside of the circle move in one direction and the men standing on the outside move in the other. Then, when the music stops, the men and women nearest each other dash to the closest chair. The man sits first and the woman sits on his lap. The couple remaining without a chair must, of course, pay the penalty." Penalties are diverse and largely subject to the inclination of the group's leaders and the inhibitedness or lack thereof of the membership. Penalties range all the way from the removal of one garment to stripping one another nude or having public intercourse in one of many positions.

"There is one game," Marlena said, "that has become practically standard in swapping circles, especially the larger ones. It's called Sheets, and since it is a piece of buffoonery and depends upon trickery, which, once perceived, will never fool anyone again, it is tried, as are fraternity absurdities, only with new pledges. The new member is sent out of the room and informed that Sheets is a strip game which calls for him or her to exercise intuition and imagination. Then 'it' returns to the room completely dressed, and fully covered by a sheet, and is told that the group has decided on an item of clothing 'it' must discard. The new member must keep discarding clothes until he or she hits on the mystery item—which happens rarely, leaving him or her nearly completely nude, since the item the group has chosen is the sheet in which they have wrapped him."

Marlena looked into her coffee cup, seeming for all the world like the respectable, infinitely desirable, upper-class matron she is, and smiled, momentarily.

"Lord, Lord, honey," she mimicked her Negro maid, "here I sit, listening to Miss Anne and Mr. Lou, talking about underground movies and card games and such, and not welcoming the talk nohow. And next thing," she looked up and shook her head slowly from side to side, "here I am, involved in an orgy, a saturnalia—anyway, a bit of high living if you know what I mean. And, well, not altogether disliking it."

The "orgy," the "saturnalia," took place at Anne and Lou's home where Dick, a fifty-year-old prominent San Francisco lawyer and his third wife, Dorothea, twenty-two, bright-eyed, cherry-cheeked, looking dainty as a doll, but in reality more worldly-wise "sexually speaking" than either Marlena or Anne, came to spend three days in the spring.

Marlena and George were also invited. They arrived

the night before the morning Dick and Dorothea were due, and slept together instead of swapping. They rose early, but to their surprise, Lou and Anne were also up. After preparing breakfast, the men went off to stock up on supplies, leaving Marlena and Anne, who had given her maid a vacation "for good reason." Anne, regarding Marlena, asked if she was uncomfortable about any of this.

Marlena could not return her gaze. "I suppose so. What makes you ask?"

"Look, with the six of us here, some may get too carried away, become too impossible. So if the going gets rough, a little scary"—it was as though Anne were thinking back to her own first such experience—"look, Marlena, the rest of us won't lose our respect for you, if you find you can't—on your first time with the six of us . . ."

"I know, but I'm looking forward to it; really I am." And in a way she was, despite her fear of the new experience.

Dorothea and Dick arrived and the afternoon was a pleasant one. After an excellent lunch, the three couples sat around the living room, listening to records, particularly an album of Arthur Rubinstein playing Chopin preludes. Later, they took a drive through Washington and Rock Creek Park.

Just before dinner a full-fledged thunderstorm broke out and the couples sat before the picture window, sipping martinis and watching the great flashes of lightning come across the sky. Dick said he hoped the storm lasted

133

through dinner and the whole night for that matter. He had always liked making love to thunder and lightning.

Suddenly, Marlena, quite drunk on martinis by now, felt that she was going to cry. No one but Dick noticed, though. "You all right?" he asked.

"I'm all right."

"You better have a drink. Hey, Lou, give the lady another martini."

He eased her into an easy chair and sat close beside her. "He fed me that silly martini as though I were a baby." "You're gorgeous," he said, while she sipped at her drink. "I didn't know that you were a queen, Marlena."

Comfortable in Dick's arms, as through a haze Marlena noticed Dorothea completely nude ("It's hot in here," she said), sitting with Lou, ruffling his hair and "touching him all over till you could hear him panting because he wanted her so badly. Drunk as I was, I could see she was completely uninhibited (she was younger than my elder daughter), and so was Lou with her. George and Anne were nowhere around, and I surmised they'd gone to a bedroom together.

"But I couldn't have cared less. Somehow, I couldn't keep my eyes off Lou and Dorothea. She undressed him and then let herself down on the floor, and pulled him till he lay there on her. I watched them: I just couldn't keep my eyes off them as she kept moaning and moving beneath him.

" 'They're having a long, hard great time, aren't they, honey?' Dick asked me. And he took the martini glass out of my hand so there'd be nothing between my body and his. Almost beside myself, hardly knowing what I was doing, I let my hands come up and touch his face. And I put my arms around his neck and clung to him.

"Even through my high, I was unable to believe I was me. I felt Dick's lips touch my lips and neck and ears and heard him say, 'Honey, you're the greatest.' He lifted me up and carried me upstairs.

"In bed, he turned me over on my back and moved against me. I knew what he would do—and, you see, I'd never done that before. I was so afraid, and, still speaking through my drunken haze, I said, 'Oh Dick, don't hurt me, please.'

"He said, 'Hurt you? Why should I want to hurt you?' And then he said, 'Oh, I see you've never had it the Roman way before. I won't do it if you don't want me to.' And he didn't—that night.

"Well, we never got up to have our dinner or anything else, and we stayed in bed till noon. And in the morning, we did have anal intercourse. I'd always thought it disgusting when I'd thought about it at all which, I can assure you, was not often. But with Dick, the new sensation was wonderful. He, like Lou, helped rid me of the sexual millstone you might say I'd worn all my life. I guess I sound like I'm on a soapbox, now, but no one can imagine how beyond belief it is to discover the joy in sex—not love and sex—*just plain sex* —at my age. And George's. In one way, that was the greatest couple of days any of us had ever had. Everyone said that. I spent two nights with Dick and one with Lou.

Dorothea and George slept together two nights, and she and Lou had their last night together. Anne was with George and Dick. We were all delighted, really.

"Then, on Sunday, a few hours before Dorothea and Dick had to leave, we had the wildest party of George's and my swapping career. We had several threesomes, you see, and neither George nor I had ever had a threesome before. First, Dorothea and I worked out with Dick. At times, Dick was the link between Dorothea and me. And at times I was the link between the two of them. At other times, of course, Dorothea was the one who lay between Dick and me.

"Then George, my George, of all people, hit upon a magnificent idea. He suggested that each man hold his own wife while someone else made love to her. You know, it was like a pipe dream come true. I found myself passionate toward the men who made love to me and thrilled with my own husband, the way he held me.

"You know, so much has happened since those days when I first felt guilty about swinging, and ashamed if my children knew. They know now." Seeing my look of sudden disbelief, she repeated it. "I told them because it's meant so much to me. I've tried particularly hard to explain it all to my daughters and their husbands. The boys are hostile, of course, but even the girls look at me like a stranger when I tell them what I do and try to show them what they're missing by not becoming swingers while they're still so young. 'All these wonderful, wonderful years ahead of you,' I say, 'if only you'd take advantage of them before waiting till you're as old as I to discover the truth.' Their retort is always the same. 'I love my husband. I love my husband.' They refuse to see. Besides, they're rather ashamed of George and me. I know they'd be humiliated if any of their friends were to discover our swinging beliefs. Not that we'd tell them, of course. To begin with, our lives, especially our sex lives, are our own business. But, like too many other people in this world, they aren't sufficiently broad-minded to think straight on this subject of sex.

"It's my fault, and George's too, that Joan and Lisa can't live unfettered as we do. But we learned, too late, to repudiate the proprieties and dictates of the Mrs. Grundys of this country. The happiness I've achieved is right within their grasp if only they'll open their minds and hearts to it. George, who's not religious in any sense of the word, can only hope for our girls' conversion. But I—I pray for it."

VIII

Money or Time No Object, but Couple Must Love Animals!

HIGHLY respected citizens like Marlena, George and their swinging companions are no longer unique in the swinging movement. During the past several years, the way-out cliques of bohemian swingers, found only in the more sophisticated cities, have been far outnumbered by people one would never suspect—couples, not only of the upper class but more significantly, of the proper middle class.

According to the Institute for Sex Research at Indiana University, there are approximately five million married couples in the United States who have exchanged partners with other married couples on some occasion, if not frequently, not only for purposes of sexual intercourse or engaging in group orgies, but also for the voyeuristic satisfaction of watching their own wives and husbands making love to others. Other authorities have estimated the number of regular swingers (excluding far-out bohemians and admitted debauchees, dissolutes and prodigals, traditional hedonists) at one to three million.

Actually the stories that have been written about swapping present only half the picture. They tell only of the satisfied swappers, seldom of the unwilling, reluctant, sad ones. The reason, of course, is understandable since those writing from the outside are generally biased and do their stories from the viewpoint of the hedonists they believe all swappers to be. And the satisfied swappers, like Marlena, consider themselves sexual revolutionaries and either don't want outsiders to know or just aren't aware of the unwilling swappers in their ranks.

But there are many, usually wives, who find the swapping life sordid and sickening but nevertheless remain for various reasons. You seldom hear about swapping wives whose lives drive them to various types of violence, ranging from suicide to assault and battery. Neither do you often hear about those wives who live their lives in fear of the day when husbands may arrange new swapping activities for them.

Only a few psychiatrists approve of swapping and some of these are swappers themselves. The majority damn the swapping philosophy more for their patients' sake than from outraged morality. Dr. Arthur A. Rhodes, the distinguished California psychiatrist, states: "You know, when a man and woman are on the verge of divorce and blame the difficulty entirely on sexual maladjustment, which, of course, it hardly ever is, I discuss with them the patterns of their marriage through the years. Usually, they've been rigid—coitus performed at, literally, planned-out times rather than spontaneously. And, of course, they've observed the *rules* of *proper* intercourse. You've no idea how many times, in my practice, I hear those two words, *rules* and *proper*.

"Naturally, then, I urge such people to give expression to their real sexual instincts, and, in fact, to explore those instincts. I try to make them see that nothing is perverse when performed with mutual pleasure. But, really, I mean this sexual liberation to be limited to the marital bedroom.

"I don't know for a fact, except through my own colleagues, but I feel I have every reason to surmise that most reputable psychiatrists and marriage counselors take a dim view of swinging as being extremely dangerous to marriage, despite all the protestations that 'it saved our marriage!' "

Reporting on cases of swingers he has known, Dr. Walter R. Stokes, a distinguished psychiatrist and Fellow of the American Association of Marriage Counselors, declares: "In each instance unhappy and tragic complications have ultimately arisen and the marriage has broken up. . . .

"[There is] the heavy risk that one of the spouses may become seriously attached to an extramarital partner, after which interest in the spouse rapidly wanes and the marriage goes on the rocks. I have known this to occur repeatedly. For these reasons, I am emphatic in discouraging this type of behavior."

These psychiatrists and others like them say that swingers are bored, jaded, sick people who need either psychotherapy or marriage counseling, not an orgy of condoned adultery. In a truly sound marriage, this view holds, a husband should be able to continue to find sexual excitement and satisfaction with his wife, and she with him. If it takes swapping to accomplish this, something is seriously wrong—either with one partner, both, or the marriage.

Most psychiatrists emphasize, among numerous negative reasons for swapping, the overwhelming one of abnormal exhibitionism as illustrated by swappers' interest in Polaroid pictures of themselves and their spouses in all manner of provocative poses. And nothing can be more revealing of swappers' hang-ups than their own media, such as their magazines. These are used by swappers for purposes of making contact with one another. A few among the most popular are: *Swingers' Life, Club Joy, Communiqué, American Club, Club Accolade, Club Infinite, National Informer, Sharon, Renaissance Club.*

Perhaps the most effective method for explaining swingers' magazine media is by anatomizing a composite issue. The cover picture is of a wife member of a swinging couple, sulky-faced with a long pageboy haircut, designed to make slits of her already narrowed eyes. Her skin pale and radiant, the black bra merely emphasizes her practically exposed attractive breasts, and the black pubic covering with a short chiffon scarf hanging from it calls attention to her powerful buttocks and upper legs. She looks, as intended, like a lion tamer who will, doubtless, stimulate the "submissive males and females" of couples who "desire to be dominated." The text bears this out: "Modern couple seeks meeting with couples with exotic tastes. Like nightclubs, photography, parties and good times. She is a brunette, hazel eyes, and 38-26-38; he is 5′ 8″ and 160 lbs. Please enclose full-length photo when answering and will reply with same."

A column describes the swingers' philosophy: "Life should be an exciting, joyous experience. Remember, you have only one life—but if you work it right, that's all you need."

There are letters, readers' comments (with photographs of nude women), ads (more photos of nude women), plus information every swinger should know: such as, the problems they may encounter with fraudulent ads. "Most fraudulent ads come from either of two species of pests: (a) The commercial operator . . . who has a product for sale and believes that placing an ad in a correspondence magazine is a good way to find customers. Their ads are almost always accompanied by a photo sold through a company specializing in pinups. (b) The would-be pornography collector. His method of operation quite often is to place an ad either as a married couple or a single woman with an interest in nudism, and then, when corresponding, request a fully nude photo that is supposed to be proof of the other party's "sincere interest in nudism."

There is advice on how to spot a phony: "Usually the photos are purchased from a company dealing in pinups and are easily recognizable. Another way is to take a close look at any vital statistics. For instance, the statement "attractive female, 38-24-36, 5′2″ and 105 lbs." sounds great until you come to the weight. A gal five feet two with those measurements would be at least ten pounds over the weight given."

There is detailed advice on how to write an ad: "instead of just saying 'male of 40' or 'female of 25,' make it more appealing by the right adjectives: 'bewitching young blonde 25,' 'tall, slim gentleman of 40.' To give your ad a real boost, have a clear, sharp, and recent snapshot of yourself published along with it. It'll usually do the trick every time."

The heart of the magazine is the ads—pages of them, with women's photos placed free. Although couples by far predominate, single men and women, evidently desirable for "threesomes" in swap clubs, are advertised too—as well as glamorously dressed transvestites.

To understand some of the ads, one must be aware of the special vocabulary of the swappers. Much of it is drawn from the jazz idiom and that of the ghetto black, the addict and the prostitute.

But the swappers' most important vocabulary, like that of all people who consider themselves members of "out groups," is the use they make of socially acceptable terms to mask their meaning and still be understood by their colleagues. For instance, "an attractive young couple" is, in the swingers' jargon, a *new* swinging couple— novices to the swinging rites. A "swinging couple" is a couple who swings with other swinging couples. What outsiders don't generally know, however, is that a "swinging couple" may or may not be married and either or both partners may be bi-sexual or homosexual. "Modern marrieds," however, are always both married and heterosexual. A "single" is a man or woman who swings alone, who attends "swap parties" without a partner to "swap" and, so, generally becomes a part of a "threesome." A "threesome," of course, is either two women with one man (this seems to be the preferable arrangement) or two men with one woman. A "foursome" may consist of two couples or three people of one sex with one of the other.

"French love," known even to many non-swappers as oral stimulation of the vulva by male or female and practiced in swap circles, particularly when new and comparatively decorous (women, for instance, who become swappers for their husbands' sakes) members are initiated. Proficient male swappers claim "French love" the most efficacious manner of captivating and thereby "soaping the way" to the women's abandonment and pleasure in sexuality with men other than their husbands. Instead of "French love" however, they use the words "French culture."

Similarly, "Roman," "Greek" and "Egyptian" culture, are, respectively, the swappers' words for anal heterosexuality, homosexuality and both bestiality and sado-masochism.

"Please, God, don't let it be too bad. Let me get through tonight."

After two years on the swapping game, in her late thirties but charming and feminine so men still gravitate to her (she must have been exquisite when she was younger and full of the sparkle she no longer has), Joanne Hyde gets a sinking feeling every time her husband arranges another weird "swap session—they're always weird"—without "troubling" to talk it over with her.

"The way it is with us," she says, "I never know whom or what we'll be meeting at some party or when it will be or where, for that matter."

Joanne, obviously shaken, picks up her glass half-filled with straight whiskey, says, "Down the hatch and over the river," downs it in a few gulps and refills it to the top. She says reflectively, "You know our swap-club meanings for Egyptian culture?"

I tell her I do.

We are sitting on the peach sofa of her moss-green living room. She reaches out for my hand. Though it is warm in the room, her fingers feel frozen, her palms clammy. "Both meanings," she asks, in her gentle, well-bred voice, "or just the sado-masochistic one?"

"Both, Joanne."

"In that case," she says half-smiling, climbing lazily but seemingly quite soberly to her feet, "I have something to show you." She leads the way on mechanical doll's feet into the library, with its high ceilings and bookshelves, and digs out from where they are buried behind the expensive leather-covered books some copies of swappers' club magazines and a red-velvet-bound diary, lettered in gold, *Bill's Journal.*

At first, Joanne riffles quickly through the magazines.

146

Not finding what she hunts, she looks more slowly and at last finds it.

"Look at this," she says, pointing to an advertisement in one of the magazines. It reads: "Experimental, fun-loving couple in thirties interested in meeting others who share their interests. Broad-minded and fascinated by all cultures, *especially the Egyptian.* Will travel anywhere to make contact with compatibles who enjoy uninhibited parties. Money or time no object, but couple must love animals and treat them kindly."

Sitting at the edge of the chair, hands folded, feet together, the silk of her dress primly pulled down past the bottom of her knees, Joanne looks demure and comfortable, despite her obvious drunkenness. All at once, though, she starts to shake, her hands, legs, shoulders, her whole body. She drops her glass. I pick it up and put it on the small table beside her black-leather easy chair. She tries to speak and can't control her tongue, although it is obvious she wants desperately to say something. She doesn't cry or make a sound, just shudders.

I move close and put my arm around her shoulders. Confused, she gropes for my hand and clings to it. She holds on hard until, at last, her hand stays firm within mine, and the firmness gradually spreads over her. "It's all right. I'm better now. Thank God that's over. And thank you a lot."

I urge her to let me get her to bed, but she doesn't want to go. She wants to talk and even manages to laugh.

"I suppose you can guess who wrote that ad."

I shake my head, knowing, and filled with pity for her. I look around the library hung with excellent oils that Bill, a successful surgeon, has painted himself. "Savagely clean," Joanne has described him—like the state of this, his favorite room. Despite the fact that he has a naturally coarse skin, Bill always looks recently scrubbed. He has graying gold hair, wavy and coarse, but as plastered-down as his quality lotion can get it. When you see him in swim trunks, you can't help noticing the same red-gold hair springing out of his forearms and muscular, heavy thighs. His face is strong as a rock but full of compassion, too, as a doctor's face ought to be. Somehow, although I have known for a long time that he has compelled Joanne to engage in the swapping activities, I still feel at ease with him, especially when sitting in the warmth of his library with soft music playing on his hi-fi.

"The bastard!" Joanne tightens her hold on my hand. "Bill was proud as a kid of that damn ad he wrote."

"He showed it to you before he sent it out?"

"Showed it to me! I'll say he did. He not only showed it to me; he wanted me to praise him for it!"

I asked what she said when he showed the ad.

"At first, I didn't say anything. I couldn't believe what I was seeing. I was horrified, realizing what Bill meant to do. But when he pressed me, finally, for the first time in all our years together, I told him how I felt."

Joanne told Bill how the whole business of swapping —"even at its most wholesome"—made her feel depressed and miserable. Every time he arranged a party,

148

even with just another couple, a "sort of civil war" broke
out in her, with her every instinct leaning toward leaving him. She said she loved him, even after all he had
done to her, but felt him vindictive toward her. Watching him make love to another woman while another
man made love to her made her feel like some sort of
prisoner. "And then I screamed at him: 'If you think
I'm going to have sex with an animal just for your
amusement, you're crazy, out of your mind.' "

At first, Bill was silent. Then with disdain he said that
if she didn't want to share in his parties he knew plenty
of "free spirits" who had none of her sexual restraints,
which "had always disgusted him," who would be happy
to accompany him to this gayest and most unusual of
parties. "That's what he said, the bastard. 'You don't
need to come if you don't want to, but, believe me, I'm
going as soon as I find the right couple.' "

Joanne snapped back at Bill: "Couple, that's a laugh!
What you really want is to rut with an animal in heat."

She smiles suddenly, a ghastly parody of her ordinary
smile.

Poor Joanne falls asleep for a few minutes. I turn out
the lamps in the hope she will rest awhile, but she wak-
ens again, completely alert. She turns on the dim lamp
by her chair. "What have you been hearing from some of
our other members about the so-called perversions swappers sometimes practice? What have you heard about
Egyptian love, for instance?"

I tell her that I have heard that true sado-masochists
are rare among swap-club devotees—most have their

own clubs—and the sado-masochistic practices during usual swapping parties are generally no more exotic than those practiced by many average couples—biting the partner or requesting to be bitten in turn. "If there's other rough treatment, it seems to stem from passion," swap-club leaders have said and then asked—logically enough—how anyone can know for a fact where passion ends and perversion begins?

"So that's what they told you?" Joanne snuffles with sudden laughter. "What'd they tell you about bestiality?"

Again, assuming that by "they" she means some of the leaders and initiators of the largest and most important swap clubs—those in California, particularly Los Angeles and San Francisco—I tell her that though there is a name for it in the movement, "it's practically nonexistent. A few have said that there've been occasional games with the host's pet dog."

"*Occasional* games with the host's pet dog! So that's what they told you? No masochism except a nip on the ear when you're making love, huh? Only occasional games with the host's pet dog," she repeats furiously. "Well, there are plenty of games with animals, particularly dogs. And if you don't believe me, read these few nice little answers Bill got to his ad."

I read. The following letter is only *one* of *fifty-four* received from all over and pasted, with great care, in his velvet-bound scrapbook; it happens to be the one he answered.

Couple Must Love Animals!

DEAR FRIENDS:

It was your ad, so I guess it's up to us to be explicit. My husband and I mutually enjoy sharing friends and experiences. We are most interested in all of the cultures, *especially the Egyptian.*

We are thirty-three and thirty-one and have found it hard to find couples who share our interests. Your ad intrigues us. We think we might possibly like to know more about you. As for us, we live alone with John, our pet collie —except he's so human, it's unfair to call him a pet. In fact, he participates in all our activities, and dear friends have said he is the *most cultured*—animal or human—of the lot of us. Actually, some of our dearest friends prefer him to us. But we don't mind since his superiority is certainly known to us who live with him, and besides, he's such a great pleasure to us both.

As for us, I am blond, 38-26-38, with blue-green eyes and a very fair skin. My husband is six feet tall and weighs 190 pounds. People consider us both most attractive; attractive enough, in fact, to be John's owners and trainers. And *that* is a *compliment.*

We are enclosing snapshots of ourselves, and John, our most precious possession, if one can call so human a dog a possession.

Hoping to hear from you in the near future, we remain culturally yours,

ELAINE AND ROBERT

And then Joanne tells how she finally agreed to accompany Bill to the party Bill had arranged with John "and his owners, lovers, whatever you want to call them."

John and his "family" live in Iowa, of all places. Robert is a writer, Elaine an artist; they are both good-looking, attractive people with many interests aside from "Egyptian culture," it would seem, since both are quite well-known in their respective fields. As for John, in spite of all that has been said about him, he seems to Joanne at first sight to be no more nor less than an ordinary collie dog except for his shiny fur. A very ordinary collie dog, who now lies curled at Joanne's feet in the living room.

Robert grins at Joanne impishly. "John's got good taste," he says. "Always did have. Since the day we first got him, he's known a pretty woman when he's seen one."

Joanne doesn't know how she does it, but she manages to smile back at Robert and to look with some affection at John. And then she notices something she hadn't seen before. Perhaps it is only her imagination, but something *is* different in this dog's eyes. This is no nice collie dog; suddenly she is afraid.

"Do you want to go to the 'little girls' room'?" Elaine asks her.

"No, no, thank you."

"Well, let me show you to your room then. I'm sure you'll want to get into something comfortable after your trip." Elaine herself wears white shorts and T-shirt, very attractive with her blond hair.

But who is to share Elaine's bedroom—Robert, or

John? No, it can't be John. It would be unthinkable to put a dog in a room with a woman guest her hosts have only just met and whose own proclivities, despite the ad written by her husband, they hadn't had time to begin to explore.

"Do get into something comfortable, Joanne," Robert repeats. "Get all those damn clothes off."

Joanne's developed instinct, which she has begun to think of as "the reluctant female swappers' syndrome," takes control, handling her fear as she follows Elaine to her room. Forget about Robert for the moment. Never even mind John. Just watch every move with Elaine, every word you say to her that might be revealing. Don't panic. Follow Elaine, wash up and get into comfortable clothes as you have been advised to do. Pretend nothing is wrong. Be careful.

"Hope this room's OK for you," Elaine says. "If not, there are a couple of other bedrooms to choose from. Just help yourself to any one you want. The pink one down the hall's mine. But I don't think you'd like that anyway. The rugs and curtains are new enough, but they're all chewed up. Chewing rugs and curtains is John's favorite occupation. Well, his second favorite anyhow. And he spends his nights in my room except when there's company."

Don't show any tension. Smile. Smile at Elaine's joke such as it is, Joanne keeps thinking to herself.

"No, Elaine," she says aloud. "I wouldn't want to change rooms. This one's lovely and the view's perfect."

"Well, then, I'll leave you to get comfortable. Take a nap if you're tired. You're sure there's nothing I can do for you before I join John and the other boys?"

"Not a thing, thanks."

"Well, then, sleep as long as you want. There's plenty of time."

After Elaine leaves her room, Joanne thinks about her last words. "You're sure there's nothing I can do for you before I join John and the other boys?" *John and the other boys.* Elaine said that. It was not a delusion of one of her drunken states. But now she goes to her bag, takes out the whiskey bottle she carries with her whenever she and Bill go to swap parties. She unscrews the cap and drinks straight out of the bottle, taking the liquor in long spurts, listening to it gurgle in her throat. Then, when she has had so much she is "almost falling on my face and can hardly make it to the bed by myself," she locks the door and lies down. But she can't fall asleep. She feels sick and weary and utterly disgusted with herself. She wants more than anything to be dead.

Getting up, she feverishly rummages through her bag for the stashed bottle. She drinks until she has finished her pint and half another one. Finally she is able to achieve what she wanted to do so badly—she passes out on the floor near her bed.

"Come on. Get up, for Christ's sake. You can't stay drunk all weekend."

She is in bed, in her nightgown, and there is a hand on her shoulder. Bill's.

"What day is it?"

"Sunday morning and we leave tonight. We've only got a couple more hours here. You didn't have to come all this distance to sleep. You could have done that at home."

Now, Joanne sees Robert and Elaine by her bed. Robert bands her arm with his iron fingers, friendly enough but strong. "Sorry, love, but you've been out all weekend and we haven't even had a chance to say more than hello. We've got to get to know you before you go home. John does too. Elaine'll help you into a robe or something."

Bill shakes his head in honest bewilderment. "I don't know where in hell she got the rest of the whiskey. I thought I'd cleaned her out after Friday night's fiasco."

Bill is very aware of Joanne's drinking and most of the places she uses to hide her supply from him. But apparently he is unaware of the perfume and face and body lotion bottles she keeps constantly filled with her fortification. He himself, like many regular male swappers, rarely drinks. As Bill and most swap-club members know, liquor impairs a man's sexual virility and can even, if he "really becomes polluted," cause temporary impotence. For this reason, particularly in large groups where a man may have relationships with several women during one night, drinking, and particularly drunkenness, are discouraged.

"Of course, Benzedrine, Dexedrine and other drugs that combat fatigue are fairly common in groups as large or larger than ours," the leader and motivating spirit of a ninety-couple California club told me. "And we also always have some pot at our gatherings, though we don't care for members who overuse that, either. Actually, we have it more for our members' curiosity than for any other reason. A man who's sexually gratified won't become addicted to pot or anything else and certainly not to the 'hard' drugs like heroin or cocaine. You know, the hard drugs which induce rather than combat fatigue are disapproved by our membership in the same way that alcohol is. We won't keep an addicted or really alcoholic couple. We want the mental and emotional awareness of our members sharpened, not dulled."

His voice grows less condemning. "Women who resort to alcohol, particularly at the beginning of their swapping associations, are, I suppose, only doing what comes naturally. They're frightened and inhibited and they use alcohol to overcome the fear and inhibition.

"Like most men, I find really drunken women repulsive, no matter how charming and attractive they may be when sober. So if a woman's a true alcoholic, I'd rather see her and her husband leave our group than stay in it."

"But suppose," I ask, thinking of Joanne, "she's joined the movement at her husband's inclination, not her own. Can you forgive her becoming alcoholic under such circumstances?"

"It's not a question of forgiveness," he answers. "The only question is—what kind of a sexual partner does a drunken woman make? I say, personally, that I wouldn't want to have intercourse with her and neither would the majority of our male members."

Martin is a well-known West Coast architect, about thirty-five, burly, bullet-headed with a sensitive face, voice and manner. And since, by his silence, he is one of the few male leaders who seems to acknowledge that some women (perhaps more than anyone knows) are in the movement because of their husbands' desire and not their own, I tell him the rest of Joanne's story.

Drunk as she was, and hard as it was for her, they made her get up out of bed and go down to the living room where John waited. Fortunately, she had a few moments alone in the bathroom—for a face-lotion bottleful of gin.

Joanne came down to the living room, fighting fatigue all the time, and, as instructed, lay down on the soft-carpeted floor so that John, who had been amply prepared for the game beforehand, could mount her for the amusement of her husband and the hosts. Then everything was over, and Bill caressed John while Elaine lay nude and waiting. Joanne buried her head in the thick carpeting in order to drown the harshness of the sounds she heard coming from Elaine and fell asleep almost immediately.

Are there any compensations for the life Joanne leads? I ask her. "None," she says, adding that she tries to conform to her husband's requests and keep her home intact for her children's sake. But her children are grown —the younger a senior in the high school where Joanne chairs the PTA; the other in college. Both, naturally are unhappy at home, and their unhappiness increases as they grow older. Marilyn is icy cold to her mother, not only about her swapping activities which she first learned of when she was almost too young to understand (Joanne, too, has found the need to tell her child—to confess?) but of everything that may concern her parents' lives together. She says, "I've gone the limit—Mom says that's a vulgar way of putting it—with a couple of boys myself. So what? I mean, once your virginity is gone, big deal; why guard it on future occasions? And I don't mind Mom and Dad knowing what I do. In fact, I laugh when I tell them, especially Mom—because Dad, I can understand him. I've taken psych courses and I know to what lengths women can drive men. And, Mom, being what she is . . . Well, I don't really blame her for everything, but you know, they're both such hypocrites when they worry about my sex life. It's a howl to hear them warning me about boys, how far to go, all that crap when they know I know about their swapping. Both of them, feeling very modern, I suppose, have discussed it with me from their own points of view. It's as though they want me to judge which one's right when I don't want to talk about any of it. Neither do I want them talking to me like good, old-fashioned, ordinary parents of a daughter who's lived in a decent environment all her life instead of one like mine. Oh, I don't mind Dad so much. But Mom's so *phony*. And, so help me, she's got the guts to ask me personal questions about how far I'd go with my boy friends and all."

Brittlely, she says, "At least, when I go the limit, it's with a boy I care something about—but her. You know once she said to me, 'That bedroom smile of yours, if I were you I wouldn't be so free with it. Boys misunderstand it and make indecent proposals. And I suppose you've been to bed with some. But how many?'" She smiles—the "bedroom smile" Joanne's talking about—and says, "I told her that after twenty I'd stopped counting."

Marilyn tries to show off, using Freudian phrases, assuming the air of a highly experienced girl. But soon she admits her façade. "I'm full of bull, too, I guess. Well, I come by it naturally from my mother."

I see tears in her eyes.

"Don't you think your father's done anything to your mother?"

"Well, I don't blame him. Yes, I do. Sure. But you don't know what it's like to have to come home every day of your life to someone like Mom. Such a damn martyr. Poor her!" Marilyn's voice is sarcastic.

Marilyn's lack of sympathy for her mother isn't surprising. A child of affluence, she can't be expected to understand her mother's difficulty in adjusting from childhood poverty, thanks to her brilliant marriage. Bill married her because she was a beauty, unspoiled, unsophisticated.

"Mom's real proud of 'having come a virgin' to her marriage," Joanne's daughter says. "If I've heard that once, I've heard it a thousand times. And, now look at her, poor thing, doing everything to keep her home together even though her husband's such a satyr." (She pronounced it "sartyr.")

"Listen, my father's no satyr. To tell the truth, Dad's the one keeping our so-called home together. He could divorce her, you know, for chronic alcoholism. But he's afraid of hurting my brother and me, losing our affection. 'If I divorced Mom,' he says, 'you would come to hate me someday. And that I couldn't stand.' Still, Dad needs sex—any man does—and she's so cold." There are tears in Marilyn's eyes, and her face has gone pallid.

"He told me about the whole thing, Dad did. He's been talking his problems with Mom over with me ever since I was a little girl, you know, and one time—oh, more than one—we talked about his and her sex life. Frankly. He told me everything, how much he'd [these next words pain her but she says them anyway] loved her when they married. Well, of course, he must have been in love with her. Otherwise, why would he have married so far beneath him?"

She looks like a little girl in her white mini-skirt and with her dark hair hanging straight and shiny over her shoulders. "I once asked Mother why she wouldn't divorce Daddy instead of forcing him to do—to the wife-swapping, for instance. She said he was forcing her; not the other way around. And I told her, 'No, it isn't true. You must like it or you wouldn't do it, wouldn't go with him!'

"She cried and said I was a little fool not to know there were plenty of reasons for her to do what Dad wanted, because he controlled everything and she loved us kids and even him so much. That last was such a laugh. So I told her, I know I shouldn't have, but I did, how Daddy'd found her frigid. I felt like a heel but I told her anyhow.

"So I asked her again why she swapped. I said, 'Don't you like it now with some of those men?' I'd keep asking her, you know.

"But all she did was to beg me to have faith in her. 'If you could just say you loved me a little, Marilyn, just say you know a little about the way I feel toward you.' "

Marilyn says that she supposes something in her should have given her comfort "when she was lowering herself to make me sick," but she found herself hating the "drunken lying woman" who happened to have borne her, who claimed she was doing for her children what she was, in reality, doing for herself.

"My mother said, 'I'll die if anything happens to this home I've worked so hard to create for you. He can be merciless, he's got such power. He can take you away from me, create a situation where I'll never see you again. Oh, I can't live without you children. If I lose you, I'll die, die.' " There is cruel amusement and complete disbelief in Marilyn's voice. " 'Die, if I don't see you again.' "

Strong language. Certainly, talking now in the days of her wine and roses, Joanne's words must seem to Marilyn nothing more than exaggeration. Marilyn's generation "dies" often after all—of embarrassment, of shame, with laughter.

Bill *is* vindictive toward Joanne. He admits it. And
there is no question that there is something macabre
about their relationship, as in the whole matter of John,
the dog. Bill himself received no sensual pleasure from
his acts with the dog. His only kick had come from
watching Joanne and John together. He knows, as well
as anyone, that in "this bit with John" he and Joanne
have crossed together into the farthest, darkest corner
of the whole swapping movement. There was a time, in
Iowa, when Joanne lay passive on Elaine's living-room
rug, that he felt he (and Joanne, of course) had lost contact with the world, were living in a nightmare.

"I thought surely that Joanne would leave me and
the children after the incident with John. But of course
she didn't. What can I do? She's got me where she wants
me. I'll never throw her out and she knows it. And she'll
never leave me, no matter what I do to her or make her
do and I know that. She'll just drink everything down
and go out and judge her garden shows or chair her PTA
meeting."

He is on his way to the hospital. One of his critical
patients, an old woman of seventy-six, has grown worse.
Gone is the cold remote look on his face as he discussed
Joanne and John; in its place are the warmth, the love
his daughter speaks of. And seeing him now, on the way
to his elderly patient, I know that no matter how he be-
haves during his off-duty hours, he has come to terms
with it. Strange? Certainly. But that is the way it is for
him. And for Joanne, too, since she is compelled by her

inner drives and compulsions to submit rather than leave him.

I knock at her bedroom door that night after I have spoken with Bill about the Iowa episode; she has asked me to stop in and say good night. She begins talking about the hell he puts her through, and then says something she had never said before—Bill's not a man but a homosexual. And unlike some understanding psychiatrists who know there can be some connection between swapping and homosexuality, she reveals implacable disgust not at Bill but at "the species. They're maniacs, cannibals, savage brutes. There isn't a decent one in the bunch and the world would be a better place if they were all dead."

"All?" I ask.

"Every goddamn one," she answers.

And incredibly, I realize, Joanne is sober tonight.

IX

"A Homosexual Is Better Off Dead"

JOHN SORENSON of Miami, Florida, is a leader of his community, a Baptist church deacon and former head of the Miami vice squad. His convictions regarding the sexual leanings and patterns of a large minority in America, its homosexuals, are on the one hand complex and on the other—backed as they are by his God and Bible—terrifyingly simple.

"I would rather see any of my children dead than homosexual." John Sorenson speaks with fervor. He is a handsome man, tall and well-built, excessively gentle in voice and manner on every other subject. And a loving devoted father to his three boys and the two sons and daughter of his second wife (his first wife died a few years ago). "And for the reason I feel there is no cure and because of the complete degeneracy of these people. They appear on the surface to be respectable, but they're the lowest forms of people. We've arrested people in all walks of life; doctors, lawyers and so forth, and once an important judge.

"This is the type of thing that gets under your skin. This fellow, this judge I'm talking of, got off. He was whitewashed through the grand jury, and this man now is back in his social circle. He's back in his church, reading the Scriptures every Sunday from the pulpit. *And we know he's a homosexual.* A very low type of homosexual, too, that preys on teen-age boys and, well, as I say, we had much evidence to put this man away, but being a former judge he got out of it, maneuvering. He intimated that we made a very sloppy, poor investigation, that the proof was very weak and that we should have known better than to arrest a man like himself, of his stature, without any more evidence than we had. And then he paraded in about forty character witnesses, talking about the judge's fine character and all this. And by the time he got through he had the grand jury pretty well sold that he was all right and he wasn't. He was a homosexual. And, well, the Bible says, it says in the Old Testament that: 'If a man lieth with another man as he lieth with woman he *should be put to death.' It's an abomination.* That's in the Old Testament and there are several quotations in the Old Testament similar to that. And also in the New Testament it says that 'these persons will never see the Kingdom of God'—homosexuals.

"There is hope, though, there's a little hope for the homosexual in the New Testament. At least that gives some hope. Because Paul says—in First Corinthians, Paul starts out by saying that 'drunkards and thieves and homosexuals and warmongers and so forth—these will never see the Kingdom of Heaven.' But then he goes into the eleventh verse and says, 'But there are some of you, ye can be saved. Ye can be sanctified to the blood of the Lord Jesus Christ.' In other words, they *may* be cured by the Grace of God. And only by the Grace of God have we ever known any of these people to be cured. But it's such a slim chance that, if I had the choice —my children are all Christians—I would say 'take them now before they become homosexuals because if they become homosexuals, they wouldn't have a chance to enter the Kingdom of God unless by some miracle the Lord forgave them and overlooked what they were. Or unless they came to the Lord—which is so rare. It's so rare for a homosexual to say, 'Lord, I'm sorry. Take me out of this life.' It happens once in a while, once in a blue moon."

I ask Mr. Sorenson if I have understood him correctly. Is he saying that because a homosexual cannot be acceptable to God, he is better off dead?

"Correct."

"And you would have him so?"

"Yes."

I ask him how he feels about other people who cannot be saved, who are not homosexuals. "Jews, for instance? Drunkards?"

According to his faith, Mr. Sorenson says, such people as Jews and drunkards cannot be saved either, but they should be allowed to stay alive because unlike homosexuals they are not "the supreme abomination in God's eyes." He asks if I know of any city that was ever destroyed because it contained, say, many drunks. "No, the only cities ever destroyed were destroyed because they had homosexuals—and they were Sodom and Gomorrah. This is the worst sin, I believe, in God's eyes. I think the sin of homosexuality is worse than the sin of murder. But, see here," and his voice lowers in intensity, "we're getting into a point of hate and this we want to avoid. We're going to lose whatever sense we have about the thing. We can't hate them. The point is to love them. Now, how do you do this? How do you love a homosexual? You love him this way. You put him in prison."

Seeing my incredulity, he says: "You put the homosexual in prison out of love not hate, because if he's ever going to have a chance it's going to be by taking him away from making other people like he is. Because this is the worst thing he can do. Being a homosexual is bad enough, but the fact that he might make someone else that way—this is the most horrible thing he can do. So you're really doing him a favor by taking him out of circulation. If you could put him in a hospital—if you had laws that would do that—but you don't. You don't have laws."

Mrs. Sorenson enters, urging me to take lemonade and cake. Sitting beside me on the sofa, she apologizes because she can't offer me something hard to drink as she once could have.

"You know," she says, "I used to be a Catholic. I'd smoke, drink, everything. But, now, since I've married John, I've become a Christian."

"Now, darling," Mr. Sorenson says benignly, "some Catholics *are* Christians." And he resumes our conversation.

I ask him how long he would keep a homosexual in prison if the law were in his hands.

"As long as I felt there was a danger of him getting out and infecting children," he says without hesitation. "Now, you take a young homosexual, say, at thirty, thirty-five. This person here is death on children. He would be suave. He's smooth. He's smart. He's got a great job. He's got a nice car. He's got a good line. He can probably get girls for the boys which will help them along the way. He is the most dangerous person. I'd keep him in prison for twenty years till he was fifty-five. You wouldn't have as much of a problem then. The kids wouldn't bother with him in the first place. He wouldn't have the attraction."

"How about homosexuals who have relationships only with each other? Two consenting male adults who have relationships, in private, with one another. You feel there *are* such homosexuals, don't you?"

"Oh, certainly, there are such. And I think it's just as much an abomination. I think the minute we start accepting this and saying it's all right—there are so many people that say, 'Well, if two men wanted to walk into another room and do something by themselves, I couldn't care less.' Well, this is not my philosophy at all. I could care because those two have got to come out of that room again and they may be schoolteachers teaching my children and I don't want any sick person teaching my children and yet there are sick people in our schools right now teaching our children. And they are mentally ill. Anybody will tell you they're mentally ill. And yet here they are teaching our children reading, writing, arithmetic, science and so forth. And their philosophies and their morals spill over."

I ask him what kind of damage a mathematics teacher, say, can inflict on a child.

Without hesitation he replies: "Homosexuals are most usually separated from those things which are morally good. I mean now, well, a child might ask a question in a class—say, in arithmetic class—he might ask a question that didn't have to do with arithmetic and this teacher can give such an answer, slant it in such a way that this child has got the wrong idea. They're subtle— the homos—they're so subtle it's difficult for me to pick an example of what I'm trying to say.

"Well, here's an example. We arrested this guidance counselor up at one of our schools a while back. This man had been involved with—I don't know how many kids. And yet nobody really wanted to do anything about it. And yet, you know, almost every kid in the school knew that he was a homosexual, because after we got to investigating it, they'd say—'Oh, yeah, he hits us on the fanny all the time and he's always telling us our pants are too tight and stuff like that, you know.' "

I ask if this is enough evidence to label a man a homosexual. Would such evidence stand up in a Miami court of law? "Haven't you ever jokingly—or otherwise—told an adolescent boy his pants are too tight, and don't many fathers kiddingly hit their children on their fannies?"

"Just his attitude made him poison. Then we finally found a kid he'd been involved with."

The "kid" was a homosexual hustler, but Mr. Sorenson seems not to condemn him, despite the fact he was after the homosexual's money, since the hustler is young. And, besides, he had been inveigled into it by the homosexual's offers of money and presents. He was ruined psychologically—which is, in its way, "moral murder, worse than physical murder and even worse than raping a child."

"I take it then, that if you were a judge you wouldn't be nearly as severe on the male prostitute as on the homosexual he hustles?"

"*Oh no.* But in court, this is always what they try to do, put the blame on the kid. The defense attorney will invariably say, 'Well, this hustler is more guilty than the homosexual because the homosexual is sick and the boy knew what he was doing.' That's silly because if this homosexual wouldn't pay for the boy, the hustler wouldn't bother with him. We've got to remember that your hustlers are fourteen- and fifteen-year-old boys while your homosexual is thirty-five to forty usually. And so you have a twenty-year age span in there. So you see, the homosexual's much more adept at molding this boy than the boy is at molding him.

". . . Besides, we've got to remember the Bible, the Old Testament. In it, the thief wasn't killed (nobody was killed and that would include the hustler) except the homosexual. God looked on him as somebody terrible you'd better wipe out before he destroys the whole world."

I pursue the point, asking that if he were responsible for writing the law regarding homosexuals, would he demand the death penalty.

"If homosexuality could be a reason for the death penalty, you would see almost a stop to this whole thing," Mr. Sorenson says with conviction.

Mr. Sorenson is one of the most sought-after speakers by neighborhood and PTA groups. The following excerpts are taken verbatim from one of his speeches before a large PTA meeting:

". . . It's not a bit dramatic to say a child's going to die in Dade County tonight, not one bit dramatic. Because he will. And you'll never know it. And this dead child may be sitting next to your child in school tomorrow morning. This is something we don't think about. This dead child. What am I talking about? I'm talking about a boy who's going to turn into a homosexual tonight. Someone's just going to flip. He's been walking that tightrope of adolescence and some homosexual will get him in his clutches and now he's going to fall off the tightrope all adolescents walk. And he's going to fall on the homosexual side. And when he falls there, he's going to try to drag everybody else in with him.

". . . and venereal disease is spread by homosexuals to an alarming degree, as you know if you read the paper today. We feel that about seventy percent is spread by homosexuals and it's not hard to figure out why, either. Because a homosexual has no morals. He will go out and he'll make ten, fifteen contacts without any problem at all.

"They say, 'Homosexuals are sick, and shouldn't be in jail.' But I don't care if they're sick or not. I don't want them around our kids. Because, no matter how much they've been punished, they're going to go out again and pick up our kids. Maybe younger ones this time."

Mr. Sorenson laughs. "Believe it or not, friends, eighty-five to ninety percent of them, homosexuals, look just like you and me. You can't tell them from us. They're not these gay types, the swishy types. They're not the feminine type. The type that'll pick up *your boy* are the *masculine* type. You won't ever know them from their appearance. They'll come and they'll have dinner in your home and you'll think, 'Isn't he charming? Isn't he a wonderful personality?' And you'll be just charmed to death with this guy. And you'll find out later on that he's been involved with your *child*. This has happened to us on several occasions. I mean, where the man has been in the boy's home. Where he actually took meals with the boy's family and then later on became involved with their child. You can't tell. Looks are no criteria at all. In fact, they're very deceiving.

". . . You know, it's legalized in England now. The great empire of Great Britain has legalized homosexuality! What happened to Rome when that happened? When Rome fell, there were fifty thousand male prostitutes walking the streets of Rome! We haven't got fifty

173

thousand in Dade County but I'll guarantee we've got two or three thousand male prostitutes walking our streets.

"We're going into the same thing Rome did. Sure. In the U.S., the great state of Illinois legalized homosexuality among consenting adults. That's the key—'among consenting adults.' How are you going to explain to your child—if he asks you—that he shouldn't commit these acts because it's wrong? 'Yes,' he says, 'but Mother, it's legal. It's not against the law. Why don't they make a law against it if it's so bad?' You say, 'This is one of the worst things a child can do, anybody can do. This can destroy your whole life. This can destroy everything.'

"He says, 'Yes, but Mom—it's legal. It's legal in Illinois. And it's legal in Great Britain.'

"No, I'll never accept homosexuals or homosexuality. What they want. This society they've got called the Mattachine. They want equal status and position. They want balance between them and us. They want us to accept them. 'We don't want to be threatened with blackmail and disgrace,' they say.

"No, I'll never accept homosexuals or homosexuality. If this is to all come to pass, then the head of the morals squad will be a homosexual." Sorenson's voice rises. "Obviously, he knows more about the thing than I do. I am not a homosexual! And I'm the only person I can swear to!

"I wonder how many in this audience tonight would like to see homosexuality legalized. Would you raise your hands please? I've got you at a disadvantage this time." He laughs heartily. "Well, you see, this business gets so serious you've got to laugh once in a while. If you don't, you die. You turn bitter. You turn sour inside.

"But to have this evil legalized, as I say, homos could be policemen. They could be—well, the President of the United States could be homosexual. He could put on his wig and his gown, go out for an evening and there wouldn't be a thing you could do about it. What are you going to do, they'd ask you, discriminate? Not if the homosexual has equal status to you; equal position. He could be President of the United States. I know that's an extreme example. But I know a fellow quite high up there. He can tell you and me what to do; he was caught in the YMCA toilet. It gets pretty close to where they can take over sometimes."

John Sorenson introduced me to Duane Barker, the man who handles all facets of investigative work for Dade County schoolteachers. He scrutinizes them all for narcotics addiction, drunkenness, absence without leave from schools they have taught in formerly, and, of course, homosexuality. He, too, was once head of the morals squad. He also served, for one year, in 1963, with the Florida legislative committee, called by most people, the Johns' Committee in "honor" of its presiding senator, Charley E. Johns, which was set up to investigate such matters as communism, fascism—and homosexuality—among people in focal positions. The Johns' Committee was called to account by most Florida newspapers for its methods of obtaining information, as well as by the Florida section of the American Civil Liberties Union, liberal churchmen and their congregations.

Duane Barker was detailed to pry out the Florida homosexuals in powerful positions, a task he executed all too faithfully—as many heterosexuals, from the director of the American Civil Liberties Union to numerous newspapermen, can testify. Among other accomplishments, he composed a brochure intended "to investigate and report on the extent of infiltration into agencies supported by state funds by practicing homosexuals . . ." Although formally named *Homosexuality and Citizenship in Florida,* the report was more popularly called "The Purple Pamphlet," a cognomen acquired, no doubt, from its mournful purple cover. Much of its philosophy echoed that espoused by John Sorenson; but what is of interest is that it has been banned in Florida and also in many other states as hard-core pornography. The reason: there are two photos, one of two males embracing passionately in the nude, and the other of a young man, nude except for a black "posing strap," with the caption: "Fetish appeal is shown in this photograph taken from a homosexual's collection. The use of the binding is frequent in artwork of this nature and an apparently strong stimulant to the deviate." "The Purple Pamphlet" is available only in those shops which sell pornography, and then only under-the-counter, unless the dealer believes you are an officer in plainclothes —in which case, it is not available at all. It defines homosexuality as "the greatest abomination." Although worded more temperately than some of Mr. Sorenson's speeches, its findings were hailed and upheld by state assemblymen and senators—until public pressure forced them to abandon the report.

Duane Barker is a tall, muscular, authoritative, good-looking and sociable man who seems to like all people—except homosexuals. Strangely, he has an awesome talent for imitating them—the "queens" as well as those who are generally unrecognizable except to each other and the few "straights" who can read their mannerisms. When young, Barker shot and killed his father, a police captain, from whom his mother had been divorced. It was a big story.

Barker says that homosexuality is bound to be more rampant in places like Florida or southern California. "There are two good reasons why 'they' [homosexuals] come here instead of going to Sleepy Hollow, Kansas, for example. The first one is the attractiveness of the climate, and the second, the anonymity of your neighbors. It's a little difficult, you know, to be a homosexual in Sleepy Hollow, Kansas, where all the neighbors can see your grandpappy's house and know what's going on in it. After a while, they've got your number. And the tar starts melting, the feathers are gotten out, you know. And so you've got to go. But in tourist resort areas, the homosexual has a real home. Now, take me. I've lived here all my life and oftentimes the neighbor's house down the street—not only don't I know what's going on there, but I don't even know the people who live in the house. They're just faces to me. I couldn't tell you their names if you asked me." He laughs, suddenly and boisterously. "I guess I shouldn't be so worried about the damn thing. But our kids—listen, you've got to worry about them. Right?" His eyes now take on more intensity, his tone becomes more measured, less spontaneous. "I'll tell you when I first became interested in the whole problem. The reason I got involved with the fags, to begin with, is because I was a juvenile officer in Dade County at a time when a juvenile officer in Brown County, a good-looking young fellow you'd never suspect, turned out to be homo. Well, I was shocked to think these people—a person like that—could get into police work. And with juveniles, too. But let me tell you, since I've gotten to know them, I think they can do anything. They're the best dupes in the world. They have the best grapevine in the world. I've heard that Mr. J. Edgar Hoover made a comment that if he had the grapevine in the FBI that the gay world has, he could fire half his agents and still get twice as much work done. And, believe me, I know what he means. From my own personal experience.

"I was in Tampa some years ago when I was working with the Johns' Committee, and I was talking with a homosexual informant and he was reading to me out of this diary he had—his own diary. And in one place in the diary, he described a massive arrest that took place in one of our major cities in the U.S., seventy-five or eighty men arrested, transvestites, homosexuals and so forth. They were up in a dance hall the police raided. They had a large meat loaf on the table shaped like a human penis and they were eating this meat loaf when the police came in.

"Well, my informant had written up everything about the raid in his diary, including the names of the major people arrested and what they were charged with, everything. And the most interesting thing about the whole business is the fellow I'm talking about wasn't even there at the time. He was in Paris. And by checking back and getting other people to help, just for the sake of curiosity, just because he wanted to know, practically every homo, every queer in Paris knew about the raid in a matter of hours, three and a half, to be exact.

"This is the point and it's so difficult to get it across to some people. It's not just the gay bars we want to get rid of so the fags'll have no place to congregate. It's not just the guy with high heels and false eyelashes. There's lots more than that to the gay world. There's that grapevine that's so fantastic.

"And here's something else, too, most people don't know. The easy way they can pull up stakes and go everywhere they want on account of the grapevine. Take the fellow who wants to leave Miami and go to California. He can find a job paying six or seven or eight hundred dollars a month in a matter of hours, while a man with a wife and two kids who just wanted to pull up stakes would have to go out and really pound the pavement.

"Well, they meet each other at their gay parties, and swap names and addresses. 'If you go to Los Angeles, see so and so.' They have a tremendous kinship. Say you're

working a big homo case in Miami and you're talking
with another detective who's also working one, chances
are that you're going to find a person that both of you
know from other cases."

Barker systematically ticks off his reasons for condemning homosexuals.

"They certainly spread venereal disease. Here in Dade
County alone, twenty-five percent of all *reported* cases
of VD came through them."

I remark that this evaluation sounds, on the surface,
somewhat more realistic than Sorenson's seventy percent. Barker looks chilly at my apparent banter. Matters
such as the homosexual's responsibility for the spreading
of venereal disease are not discussed lightly. Then he
laughs, quickly and nervously. "Well, you've got to admit the thing's a little bit shocking, either John's figures
or mine. I mean, I may be old-fashioned, you know, but
it's my belief that when you catch the bug doing what
comes naturally, OK. But the pansy way . . . And besides, if you consider the unreported cases, John's figure may be more or less right at that."

He says you can blame all those unreported cases on
the homosexual doctors. "I would say there are dozens
of them, hundreds of physicians who are homosexuals
right here in Dade County. And I dare anyone—a homosexual doctor or anybody to challenge my figure. I
dare anyone. There are hundreds of them and it's sickening."

But how does the homosexual find a physician who is
also a homosexual? I ask.

"How?" Barker repeats. "Well, I'll give you one instance. He goes to a party in Miami Beach or in Hialeah, the fellow with VD. At the party, he meets this doctor. And, of course, he knows that, being a homosexual himself, he's going to protect him if he goes to him as a patient. In other words, he knows the doctor is not going to send an official report on him to the U.S. Health Department which operates with the state health department. So he'll go to a homosexual physician who'll treat him and not report him. And all the time the only thing the Health Department official is saying: 'Look, we don't care who you are but let us know your contacts so we can get to them and treat them.' But they won't. So you can't link the spread with them like you can with anyone else. I mean, even if there was a homosexual who was willing to cooperate with the health officer, he couldn't. Like if he's a 'johnny queen.' I don't want to insult your intelligence but the fellow who frequents toilets, public toilets, is called a johnny queen. And he will cohabit with maybe fifteen or twenty men in a day's time through a two-inch hole in the toilet partition. Well, even if he were the best of guys and the most reliable of citizens and really wants to cooperate, how is he going to describe a man standing on the other side of a partition when all he sees of him is his private parts? So, even if he wanted to cooperate, how could he? And yet the disease can be transmitted orally. He can transmit the disease fifteen or twenty times in one public toilet in one day."

He says these physicians are known to the police but

not sufficiently known so that they can be prosecuted. "What I mean by 'known' is this. You're a vicer chasing homos and you confiscate fourteen address books in four-teen different homosexuals' apartments or homes. They all have Dr. Jones' name in them. And then let's suppose you raid a fag party and see this same Dr. Jones sitting on a sofa with his arm around a couple of fellows wear-ing falsies. Then you'd have to—I mean, you couldn't avoid knowing this fellow's one of them. Right? Right." He nods. "But you can't prosecute them, you see. You go to the D.A.'s office with all the information you've got on this Jones fellow and he tells you to go out and get more information; get vital information before he can even undertake to prosecute the case in court. Well, there you are, stymied. And the whole thing's ridiculous. You've been working your head off for nothing while Dr. Jones is getting rich and his pansy patients are hav-ing themselves a ball because they know the law can't touch them.

"They're a menace to us all. Not just where health's concerned . . . But the money businesses lose on their account. Man." He touches his handkerchief to his nose. "Insurance companies are scared to issue them policies. I mean the rich homosexuals, the ones who live, let's say, in mansions, great big houses in Coral Gables. They invite a few boys to spend the weekend. Hustlers, weight-lifting boys. They're the ones who appeal to them. The whole bunch has a few drinks and so forth and all of a sudden one of the boys knocks the food out of the rich fag and takes his hi-fi, suits, clothes and all the money lying around. He cleans him out.

"Now the homosexual may not know these boys really, because he just picked them up for the weekend. But he's not a cretin or an imbecile. He knows the gay bar where he met them. And chances are that if he'd describe them to the insurance investigator and the investigator'd go to the bar, talk to the bartender, he'd find out the boys' identities. Because they're probably habitués, coming to the same bar to score night after night. So the fag's got all sorts of leads for both the insurance companies and the police.

"But when he finally calls the police, he's sitting there with a bandage across his head. And when you ask him how he got hurt, he tells you. 'Mmm hmm,' " Mr. Barker's teeth click with contempt. "He tells you he fell down the steps in his house. The window is broken and all these items are gone. But all he did was to fall down the steps."

He twists a letter opener on his desk. "And when you ask him how come all these things are missing, and how come the window's broken, he doesn't know a thing about it. He was out when everything occurred. All he can think of is that a burglar must have broken in.

"You know, he'd never have called the police except that it's required in order to satisfy the insurance company for all these items the burglar supposedly took. But when the time comes to provide the policeman with a lead, he can't. He can't afford to give you the lead,

183

put the finger on the hustler, especially if he's young. Because if he does and the kid's willing to make a statement about the reason he picked him up, why then he's got a real problem. So I'd hate to venture a guess as to how much the insurance companies in this area alone lose every year on account of the homos. But it's millions of dollars. Oh, God help us. Millions and millions. And the more queers come in, the more they're going to keep on losing.

"And credit card people, the homos are their biggest headaches. I'm willing to bet anything that if they know a man's queer, they won't have anything to do with him. Hustlers are always looking to steal their credit cards, grab them so they can go off on a big toot. And the queer won't tell any more about who steals his credit card than he will about other stolen items because he might have engaged in a sexual act with that boy before he stole the card."

Like Sorenson, however, Duane Barker places the responsibility for the hustler on his mark, the homosexual.

He draws a deep breath and says, "If only our area wasn't so attractive to fags. When I say 'attractive,' I'm talking about all the hedges we've got, the greenery. Now this may sound like a small thing but it isn't to homos, who want privacy. Any house in which you find homos living, you'll also find a lot of shrubs, hedges, trees, a dog in the driveway. Anything they can put up to keep people going by from getting tag numbers from the cars they have in their driveways when they're having parties. And they're always having parties."

When I ask why people's license tag numbers should be taken merely because they are attending a party at someone's house, he seems not to hear.

"The drugstores in the downtown area are lousy with them. You can't go to the little boys' room without having three or four people proposition you on the way.

"And the gay bars. All the fairies in Dade County would move in a hurry if we refused to tolerate their bars. Homosexuals will move to a town five hundred miles away if they know it tolerates gay bars. Now you might like a cocktail once in awhile. You may have a favorite spot in town that you like to go to with your husband and have a couple of drinks, but if they'd shut the place down you wouldn't have a heart attack. You'd go someplace else. But the homo, if the chief of police says, 'I don't want gay bars operating in my town. We're going to close the gay bars. They're places of assignation. Men make dates with men in them. They swap pornography, swap doctors' names. We don't want them here.' The homos'll go crazy if their favorite place is closed.

"A fag will give up a job, a home, everything, to move to an area that stands for homo bars. And I don't know why this is so difficult to get across. So many say, 'It's right to have homo bars so you can keep an eye on them, know where they're at.' Well—that's nothing but a lazy police chief's alibi, that's all it amounts to. All safecrackers are not going to go to the same place. All rapists are not going to use the same girl. It's foolish, that argument of 'We'll know where they're at!'

"Oh, some people are willing to come out in the open. The interior decorator. The poodle trimmer. Sure, but all you have to do is look at them and you know what they are anyhow. Do you think they care though? No indeed, you don't find many interior decorators trying to convince the world they're straight. 'If I'm gay, so what? I'm making a mint. Who cares?' But the gay vice-president of an insurance company, a guy with a big insurance company can't admit what he is. And he's the one you've got to look out for as far as your juveniles are concerned."

Suddenly he gets caught up by the heat of his emotion. "These people who get all shook up, nervous and angry about the gay people and civil rights. 'Let them be out in the open,' they say, and there won't be any problems. That's as much as they know about the whole thing. 'No stigma!' they say. 'No blackmail!' Fiddlesticks.

"Approval of consentual acts between adults! My God, how can they be so stupid? Don't they know that all their ideas can lead to is perversion of our children? Don't they *care* what happens to the children of this country, to the young people? Don't they *care* whether they're protected or not? *Don't they even love America's kids?*"

X

"Don't Have Him Another One-Night Stand!"

"IF A man does not keep pace with his companions, perhaps it is because he hears a different drummer. Let him
step to the music he hears, no matter how measured or
faraway."

These words from Thoreau were quoted to me by
Harold L. Call, long-time president of the Mattachine
Society of San Francisco, a local branch of a national organization of homosexuals. Devoted to the homosexual
cause, the Mattachine Society is dedicated to securing
for homosexuals their constitutional rights and instructing them on their duties to society (such as how to conduct themselves with juveniles, or their responsibility
to cooperate with the Health Department in helping
obliterate venereal diseases). The Mattachine Society
of San Francisco, for example, operates a broad social
service department. It makes referrals to religious and
therapeutic counselors for homosexuals in need of them,
finds them jobs and homes, deals with draft and veterans'
problems, offers rehabilitation aids to persons out of

hospitals and correctional institutions, and aid to potential suicides—a frequent problem in the homosexual community.

I am in Harold's office during the annual ten-day national assembly of all homophile organizations. While I wait for Harold (no mincing walk, no rotating thin hips or well-plucked eyebrows), a young Negro boy of eighteen, a shy smile on his face, walks into the office. Harold was expecting him and has told me a little about him.

"This kid," he said, "was referred to me by Officer Blackstone who's with the community relations division of the police department. He's a *keptive*, not a captive, a *keptive* to two older men who use him sexually and keep him comfortable. Now, though, he wants out of the alliance. He wants to be on his own. Officer Blackstone says he's a great kid, with ability, and to do what I can for him. If he hadn't been referred by the police department, though, I doubt we'd have accepted him."

Automatically I asked why.

Harold said merely, "You know why."

And, of course, I did know. Anyone who knows heterosexuals' attitudes regarding homosexuals and juveniles would have to know. The trouble, plainly and simply, is that the heterosexual community—the majority of whom have never met homosexuals face to face—regard all homosexuals as "swishes" with dangerous desires for juveniles and ever ready to make sinister advances to anyone exposed to them. This ancient belief

has plagued countless generations of homosexuals before
it caught up with Harold Call.

"Please have a seat," Harold tells the boy, John, who,
still smiling diffidently, sits on the edge of his chair.

"I know something about you," Harold says frankly.
"Officer Blackstone told me. But if there's anything else
you'd like to tell me yourself—anything about yourself
that will help me help you more . . ."

John lowers his head from Harold's open gaze, as
tremulously he tells his story. He had come to San Francisco from New Orleans only recently. He left home
after graduating from high school because he had been
unhappy there and also because he had finally faced his
homosexuality. . . .

He talks very slowly and shyly, sometimes stopping altogether. Harold tells him to take his time. He does not
have to talk at all; the Mattachine Society will do all it
can for him anyway. "I know," Harold says, "speech
hurts sometimes."

No, John answers, putting his hands over his eyes
as though to rid himself of some memory; silence hurts
him more than speech does. He wipes his forehead and continues. Having little money and not knowing where to
turn, he had been relieved when the two sugar daddies
on the prowl had picked him up and taken him home.
His eyes shine with moist appeal. For what? Sympathy?
Understanding?

Harold certainly understands. He understands, too,
that at a time like this, what John needs is a gesture of

189

reassurance. Had I been sitting across from John, I would have reached out for him, but because Harold is a homosexual he can offer the consolation of words only.

Gradually, John thaws, loses his diffidence. Thanks to Harold's extraordinary sympathy and understanding, he tells in detail his life with the two sugar daddies. John says that they had given him a boat and a car and more money than he could spend. But, and this is said with vehemence, none of those luxuries could make up for the loss of his independence.

Always suffering from a severe inferiority complex, he finds this present alliance only intensifies his insecurity; sometimes he feels his whole life is unreal. He had had numerous solitary dialogues with himself before he decided to make the break with his sugar daddies. On the one hand there had been the siren singing of living on in comfort with the two men who seemed to want him so desperately that they would do anything to keep him; and, on the other, common sense told him that the "whole bit was doomed to failure sooner or later."

He knows other young homosexuals who seemed to get satisfaction from the material things their sugar daddies showered on them, yet he asked himself what was the use of having left New Orleans and come to San Francisco to be as dependent here as he was there.

Finally, he had gritted his teeth and gone to seek help in getting a job, any job just so it would enable him to stand on his own feet.

"Good!" Harold says confidently. "You came to the

right place for finding that job, son. I can assure you you'll be OK."

John looks up. There are tears in his eyes.

Harold was in a blue funk the first time we discussed his homosexuality, and life as a homosexual; taut, restless, angry with himself because he hadn't been able to raise sufficient funds that month to keep the San Francisco Mattachine Society running. And the Mattachine Society, understandably, is an obsession with Harold.

"The ones who can help you [successful homosexuals] won't because they don't want to be identified. They're what we call 'closet cases,' hiding and scared to death of exposure. And the ones who need you—and how they need you!—can't help. They're too poor." Angrily, he said, "But just let one of them, one closet case, get into trouble and he comes running to us for help."

It is sad to see Harold in this kind of dark mood. "I'm sorry to be such a drag tonight," he said, finally, "but I swear to God, I'm mad all over. Mad! It's too absurd our not being able to get money from our own people because they're afraid someone will recognize them." He held his hands stiffly so that the veins rose. "They've carved out their nice little comfortable niches. They don't care about police brutality toward the homosexuals they pick up, they don't care about employment of homosexuals or their civil rights. If you're a homosexual who hasn't made it like they have, you're a lowbrow, a bum. And to *hell* with you."

Harold Call is, in many ways, one of the fortunate homosexuals. So many homosexuals try unsuccessfully to tell their families about their sexual orientation. And many, particularly those bred in the rural Midwest where Harold was born and brought up, have been thrown out, disowned by their families.

"It's not like that at all with my family and me," Harold says. "My mother, in particular, has been very understanding about everything. In fact, she's a member of Mattachine and contributes to it regularly. And we're very close, even more so now than before she found out I was a homosexual. I guess I got the drop on both my parents because I didn't make any bones about what I was. You know, if they'd disapproved or tried to make me feel guilty, I would have abandoned them before they did me. Once they became aware and started to question me, I told them clearly and simply what my score was and I didn't intend to change for anything or anyone, including them."

Harold was born on a farm in northern Missouri, near a county seat of some seven thousand people, the first child of his parents' marriage. He smiles. "In a sense, I was a disappointment to my mother. Not me, exactly, but my gender. She was mad to have a girl and here comes me instead. I remember, while I was growing up, overhearing her talk to her friends about it, other young housewives. And I was conscious of other things at a very early age. I had long hair. I was very blond as a child, a towhead. And Mother liked to comb and fix my hair. Usually she made it into finger curls.

"She did the same for my two younger brothers. And she's still so fond of our baby pictures in which we all wore white dresses and had finger-curled hair. You can't imagine it."

Three more different men than he and his brothers could never have been born, Harold says. "Actually, my brothers and I grew up much as did other boys in northern Missouri."

Harold credits Dr. Evelyn Hooker, professor at the University of California, who has done much research among homosexuals, with helping him dredge up early experiences and reactions. He remembers, for instance, when he was four years old and he and a little girl of his own age took off their bathing suits on a secluded beach and "sat around naked. We didn't do any fondling or anything like that. Just examining one another was a remarkable enough experience, and I still remember my feelings. I was utterly confused, had so many questions about why she didn't have a penis like me and I didn't have a vagina like she did. Why were we two so unlike one another?"

He wanted to talk to his mother, "to ask her a million questions," but he knew intuitively that he could not.

By the time he was eight, though, he had gathered courage enough to ask her where babies came from. He laughs. "That eighth year was a real milestone for me. I learned from the other kids that there was no Santa Claus and that babies weren't brought by storks."

His mother's explanation about where babies came from still beguiles Harold: she explained that babies grow inside their mothers until they are ready to be born. "And when the proper time comes, God opens the door in the mother, prepares the door so the baby can come out into our world."

"Didn't she ever tell you about the father's role?"

"I guess she wanted me to think the mothers were self-sufficient and didn't need the fathers for anything relating to the children."

He had believed her for a while.

"But then, I found out from other kids that Mother and Dad had to do something together and that something was named by a four-letter word . . . and then I was ten."

"What happened when you were ten?"

"I was introduced to masturbation by some older kids I ran around with. And I didn't like it the first time. It just seemed sort of irritating, that's all. I don't know whether I was reacting out of guilt but that's just the way I felt."

He was ten, too, when his mother and father were divorced. "When I talk about it to this day, I feel like crying."

He and his brothers had always felt an atmosphere of tension around the house, he says. "Of course, we didn't recognize then what it meant but we do now. I guess nowadays and even then, when I was growing up, those in educated and sophisticated circles would label Mother frigid. I remember now that I heard rows and fusses coming from their room. Obviously, it was because he wanted to have intercourse and she didn't. And after the arguments were over, I'd hear my father step out on the front porch and leave it dark, never turn on a light. He would stand out there alone for a long time. It's obvious to me now that he was masturbating. He had to do something about his sexual tensions."

After twelve years of such an unsatisfying marriage, he became bitter toward her and the snarling arguments between them came out of the bedroom and into the open. They didn't argue about sex, they argued about infinitely smaller matters; but it rocked their children's world all the same to see their parents breaking apart in front of them.

When his father turned to another woman who was as sexually frustrated as he, Harold says his mother's pride and fundamentalist convictions—sex for pleasure instead of procreation was a sin—"made her divorce my father." Because Harold's father loved his wife and children and because of his violation of the moral standards which he and his wife both shared, he reluctantly consented to a divorce. Harold's mother was awarded custody of the children.

"I remember," Harold says, "how torn we all were, because we loved both our parents. And after a while, Dad, probably figuring that Mother might relent and take him back, sued for us and won. And he had a point, at least in the eyes of that country judge who presided over the case. You see, Dad alleged that Mother was a woman of poor moral character because she'd been see-

ing a man whom she still sees and who has been her life-
long admirer. They're about the same age and grew up
on neighboring farms.

"You would have to have been brought up in a rural,
rock-ribbed Baptist community," Harold says, "in order
to know the conscience there that *always* wins out over
logic. That's why they thought they had something on
Mother. You see, she'd accepted certain gifts from the
man and that was enough to mistrust her testimony.
Strangely, I don't believe anyone tried to prove she'd
been to bed with him. That didn't enter the picture. She
was playing around with a man without being married
to him, and that was enough to condemn her in their
eyes."

After they had been taken from their mother, Harold
and his brothers went to live on a farm with their pa-
ternal grandparents. "I guess you could say I was shoved
from pillar to post. When it came time for me to go to
high school, I was sent to live with my uncle and aunt
near St. Joseph, a town of about seventy-five thousand,
big by comparison with my own hometown. They were
childless and I was like their own. They actually put me
through high school.

"But my aunt was always suspicious of people, anybody and everybody. She wouldn't trust a soul. She always thought people were trying to steal from her. Oh,
it was awful when apples were in season. She was always
on the lookout for people who would try to steal apples
from her trees. I guess it's amazing I grew up free from
her kind of suspicions about people."

All the same, she limited his development. "She insisted, while I was going to high school, that I be at home exactly when classes were over, so I had a very limited social life with boys and girls of my own age. I never dated like the other boys did. But in all honesty, I didn't care to date—girls, that is. No, even back then." Actually he suspects he welcomed her coddling because it prevented him from facing himself before he was ready. "And she did allow me to stay late for extracurricular activities. I had a part in every school play, and I was on the school paper." But participation in athletic activities was a very different story. Whenever he was asked to join in he could always say his aunt wanted him at home. "But, seriously, she was crazy, wild, if she didn't know where I was for a couple of hours.

"When I received a first-year scholarship to the University of Missouri, my aunt was just as proud of me as my own mother. Dad drove me to school and I guess I was the poorest kid in the whole place. All I had was a whole ten-dollar bill, all of that. I got a big thrill out of figuring ways and means of seeing myself through the university."

His tuition was paid by his scholarship, and he got room and partial board for serving as companion to a doctor's son, years younger than he. Other necessities he earned from the work he turned out on a small printing press. "I got pocket money from a little-theater group I printed for.

"It wasn't a bad life. Actually it was a challenge. In order to live, I had to be inventive." He lingers over the word. "I could have gone on with that life until I finished school. But then the Second World War started, and they inducted me into the service."

A homosexual's fears when he is inducted into the Army are intense. The awful specter, Harold says, that haunted him day and night was not of being killed or having, himself, to kill, but rather that his secret would be given away. How would he react in the presence of so many men? He would have to quench his natural impulse. But could he?

"Oh, how I dreaded the thought of the Army. I kept thinking to myself, 'Dear God, I hope they find something wrong with me and muster me out before they even get me in.' And then, you know, it was a funny thing, but the closer we got to the induction center, the more my thinking and reactions changed. I was half-sick with terror they *would* find something wrong. I'd been given a big send-off party by my friends at the university. And right in Missouri there, I was the one they'd put in charge of the whole contingent of draftees from our area. So I was fearful as hell. 'My God, what if I don't pass the test?' "

Fortunately, thirteen weeks after his induction, something happened to change all that. "I was sent to officers' candidate school in Fort Benning, Georgia. I took a crash course and became a second lieutenant, and believe it or not of the cynical 'bitch' you see before you today [I had to laugh at Harold's use of the homosexual word 'bitch' in relation to himself], I was awed, overwhelmed by the responsibility my country had thrust upon me. And I knew from the moment they told me I was going to Benning I'd be able to overcome any impulse. On account of the responsibility. I took it seriously, I can tell you."

Harold served thirty months overseas and became a captain with duty in the Pacific. After the war was over, he returned to school under the GI Bill of Rights. "In the meantime, Senator McCarthy was raving and ranting and really put the score on homosexuals, good, bad and indifferent. And on April 1, 1950, All Fools Day, the Mattachine Society was organized. Really, it represented the first little ray of hope for many people so troubled, feeling themselves so much outcasts and rejects. They didn't know they could band together and thus gain strength from one another. They didn't know the potential of their organized strength, as we know it today, until Mattachine was organized. The word 'Mattachine' by the way, means 'little fool.' The little fools of the Middle Ages entertained royalty; they were the court jesters.

"The Mattachine Society was a defiance of heterosexuality, a flaunting by homosexuals of those who looked down upon them. It said, 'I am what I am, because, with all your power, with all your disgust, you've never found a way to stop me. And a hell of a lot of you will drive your children to do what I do. You may not be worse than my parents who had a hand in helping me to choose the road I did—but who says you're so much better?' And Mattachine headquarters was also a place where frightened people could relax and laugh together. Well, thank God, we've come a long way since then. We still laugh but we also engage in important activities. And we've become nationally known, not just because of our work with homosexuals but also because of our involvement as citizens. In this respect we operate much as 'straight' organizations do."

Harold knows exactly when and where his recognition of himself as a homosexual began. He was thirteen when he masturbated for the second time with a cousin, a year older.

"I didn't feel guilty about it in spite of all the sermonizing I'd been exposed to all my life either. Actually those sermonizers never did hit the basic facts about me. My being gay, I mean. I don't think it'd ever entered their minds that a boy could be gay.

"Certainly the cousin with whom I masturbated wasn't gay. Our relationship was a passing thing with him—an adolescent thing. And I knew it. I also knew it was different for me. I had girl friends in school but they never— well, I enjoyed them but I didn't want to date them; neck and pet. And I think, in fact I know, that the girls, at least some of them, sensed that there was something different about me.

"I also brought out the son of the doctor with whom I lived while I was at the university. But our relationship was very much like the one I'd had with my cousin. Just a playtime thing for him. And I never felt lonely or exploited. Not with either my cousin or the doctor's son. All three of us got what we wanted and needed—release from physical pressure. We all knew the score. I was no more starry-eyed about them than they were about me."

The story sounds familiar, because I have heard it from so many homosexuals. Harold, in his forty-nine years, had had up till then 1,953 sexual contacts with men. This is absolutely correct, he says, because he has reconstructed all his experiences for Dr. Hooker, kept an accurate record.

Harold's blandness mocks my shocked tone. "I said experiences, not orgasms. Half fulfillment is better than none, you know."

"Then you couldn't have had a real love affair could you? Ever?"

Harold replies promptly. "Oh, but I have. In fact, I've had seven—what I would consider, by gay standards, love affairs. I was certainly emotionally involved while they lasted and so were my lovers. Now, with three of them, there was a considerable difference in our ages. I knew from the first that I was more an uncle and mentor to them than a lover fulfilling their erotic needs. Yet, thinking back on it, I guess I fulfilled some of their erotic needs too. My sexual contacts with these seven were not equal in intensity either for them or me. Sometimes, they needed me more than I did them, and sometimes it was the other way around. . . . But from where you sit, by 'straight' rather than gay standards, I've had one honest-to-God love affair. One," he repeats, turning away, and it seems a long time before he faces me again. "We lived together for eight years." He adds, with desperation, "I haven't got any more cigarettes."

I ask him to tell me about the man, what he did professionally.

Harold's face has grown very pale. "Nothing. He did almost nothing to earn a living. He'd joined the Navy when he was seventeen and left it by the time he was eighteen and a half. The Navy considered him partially disabled and paid him disability benefits because he was released with an anxiety neurosis. And as he grew older his anxieties increased. Life became more complex and his responsibilities . . . truthfully, he just wasn't able to face life bravely. He grew more and more dependent on Mother V.A. I know our life together and his homosexuality had little or nothing to do with it. But he's in a mental hospital now, drawing total disability."

Harold's voice had taken on a trancelike quality. "But I loved him and he did me. For eight years and then off and on, whenever we could get together we did. I'd visit him in the hospital whenever I could, and sometimes he'd get leave and come and stay with me."

"If he hadn't had to be hospitalized . . . ?"

"Oh, we'd still be together . . . I know we would. I'd have done anything," he says, "anything to help him. But there was nothing . . . the doctors all said that the best thing for both of us was for me to give up and forget him. If he could come back, even now, he could have everything I've got. And without asking for anything in return.

"Maybe my reason for feeling that way, wanting to give without caring if I get in return, will reveal too much

about me. But all my life, I've been attracted to the people who need me. Besides," Harold says, "you'd have to
be gay yourself to know how much someone like me
would value a long-term relationship; so different from
what heterosexuals would settle for. Homosexuals' relationships, generally speaking, are a wearisome, nightly
routine of production-line sex, pantomime of buying and
selling. There are some pickups, of course, who will
spend a night together without an exchange of money,
true. But you know it's all over in the morning—you'll
never see each other again. Perhaps I didn't tell my story
about my lover straight," Harold says, "but there were
so many good times we had together, so much closeness
and peace." With none of the loneliness Harold feels so
often now.

Harold took me on a round of gay bars in San Francisco one weekend. A few were elegant: their clientele
mostly made up of couples who had been living together for a long time. These long-termed marrieds be-
haved as married heterosexuals do. Mostly they were
with friends, as well and conservatively dressed as they,
and like the highly respected members of the community where nobody knows or would believe their sex patterns. Little flirtation went on, sedateness was the key-
note. The man who guarded the door was wearing a dinner jacket and spoke with an English accent. The small
cocktail lounge was furnished with gilt tables and chairs.
The meal was perfect, the staff gracious. The restaurant
was very discreetly run. The only difference between it

and other restaurants was the clientele—you rarely saw a woman. And many of the customers were celebrities. Everyone and everything was discreet, even the pianist softly playing blues and jazz.

I listened to the patrons' conversations. The talk was mostly of homes, boats and long overdue vacations. A man at the next table said he had been working hard and needed a break. "If you'd like, Jack, we can spend part of the winter in Bermuda." But Jack loathes Bermuda. "It's full of all those dreadful Miami Beach types," and couldn't his companion "please think of somewhere else to go." "Like what?"

"Well, like Paris, for instance," Jack replied. The companion said in a lowered voice that I managed to catch anyhow, "But, darling, Paris is dreadful in the wintertime. All that snow and cold, you might as well be going to New York." Jack's companion laughed at the comparison. "Dearest, you do lack a sense of social distinction." He laid a hand on Jack's shoulder. "Well, what about Acapulco then?" Jack brushed away the smoke of his cigarette. "Acapulco? What do you want to be, sweet? One of the beautiful people?"

I turned away and listened to the conversation at another table. "I'm a fool. Romantic. I believe in people," one man said. "Not a fool; just empty and unsatisfied till now," his companion replied persuasively.

One man sat alone, at the edge of the group. He was older than the others, in his late fifties or early sixties. He wore a hearing aid and pince-nez. Although the man was by himself, he was not here to make a pickup, Harold told me. People come here with their own lovers or, on rare occasions, like this, alone. But he had no thought of finding a companion in this place. Harold smiled. "Let him just give someone a fraction of a wink and there'll be trouble."

"What's he doing here then?"

Harold pulled out a rose from the vase on our table. "Oh, he just wants to be among the beautiful people for a while." He replaced the flower in a vase at a different angle. "Unless, of course, he's new to this town and doesn't know the true clientele of this restaurant. Although he'd have to observe it, stranger or not, pretty soon. Certainly, there isn't a hustler in this place. I mean, that would be obvious even to a moron, wouldn't it?"

Harold grew melancholy speaking of pickups and the whole mood of his speech changed. "Oh, God, there's nothing sadder than a lonely gay guy in a strange town, dreary in the late hours. Say I'm in New York and looking for company and don't know where to go. So I'd gravitate, naturally, to Times Square. But that's no place to go unless you're a guy who doesn't mind being a score, who's looking for a hustler. Times Square is their beat in New York; the beat of permanent New York hustlers as well as the ones who are here today and gone tomorrow. The ones you see one night who've gotten busted the next. The ones who just got tired of the Times Square scene the night after you've had them and have gone on to Florida or California or Mexico. You've had them one night and they've gone the next. You didn't expect them to tell you their plans, of course, or say good-bye any more than you'd expect it of a prostitute.

"So lots of gay men learn to take being a score. But suppose a person can't. Certainly, it bugs his pride to have to pay for what every person wants as free from the person who loves him. But there's more than dignity at stake for the gay score when he goes with a hustler. His bankroll, I mean. Scores get rolled a lot more often than tricks do."

Harold said that hustlers often beat and murder their scores for many reasons; money is only one. Hustlers can be bug-eyed on alcohol or blasted on narcotics so they are not themselves. More often, though, homosexual hustlers find themselves seized by a powerful guilt, a sudden, unexpected, scorching shame, coming on them while they are with their scores. Besides, as anyone knows who has a real acquaintance with scores, many would rather think of themselves as male prostitutes who can never be aroused by their customers than as flagrant homosexuals who have chosen this way of making a living. Their denial mechanism must of necessity be stronger than other peoples'. They must display a cool, especially to one another. With their customers there is also a hostility that can only be expressed in doing overt harm to them.

Often, they talk together as did Mike, seventeen, and Red, nineteen—two New York hustlers I know—after Red had returned from a room with a score.

"So," Mike asked derisively, although he, too, had

been waiting to score. "How'd you make out with the fruit, baby? Enjoy yourself?"

"Enjoy myself? You must be kidding!"

"Well, what happened?"

"Dig, man, I only went with him because he'd give me a tenner if I just let him blow me a little." Since to the hustler being a passive partner for the sake of money has no connotation of homosexuality—unlike any kind of mutual activity—most claim to stop at "being blown" which "leaves them cold." Red, though, embellished his story, probably because of Mike's taunting. "So we go to his room and he blows me. 'OK,' I say, 'where's the bread?' He says, 'Just a minute.' And next thing he's naked on the bed on his belly and says he'll give me another ten for doing him like that. Like I'm some fucking fruit, you know. And when I see he's that way—all I want is to get my ten bucks and split. So he says, 'I was like you once and now look at me, playing the other side of the game. What the hell, people change, and someday you'll be where I'm at.'

"So that depressed me . . . I mean, that he could think I was a fruit like him and would end up an auntie. Man, I was in an absolute depression."

"Bad scene," Mike said. "Bad scene." Then, contemptuously: "I bet you never even clipped his wallet." The implication of the challenge was not lost on Red—since he didn't overtly hurt the score he is as gay as the score implied.

Like a gang leader looking for a rumble from a rival, Red lost his cool. "Oh, didn't I just!"

"And what was in it if you clipped it?"

"The ten he promised me. And a C besides."

"Let me see the bread."

"I don't have it here."

"Well, what'd you do with it then? You only left here half an hour ago. You couldn't have spent it up."

Red thought hard. "I went right to the P.O. and sent it to my old lady."

"You think I'm nutty or something? I know you don't have a wife."

"My old lady is my mother," Red said. "I never said anything about wife."

"I don't even think you got a mother *living*."

"You don't think! What right you got to think anything about who I got and who I don't? I'll show you anyway." He removed from his wallet a photograph of a skinny, elderly, thin-haired lady and tenderly passed it to Mike.

"Mmm. So you got an old lady. That don't mean you go clipping C's just to send to her."

"How would you know that either?"

"Listen, if you did send the bread to your old lady it was for one reason." Mike, on the attack, said the most hurtful thing one hustler could say to another: "You know you're getting old and the scores won't want to pay for you. What'll you do then? You'll go back and live on your old lady, that's what. So, if you did send her the C like you said, it's only to get on her good side now while the getting's good. Before you get too damn old."

The shaft hit home. For to Red and his like death *is* the loss of youth.

Red no longer had the heart for quarreling and left without a word. When he was gone, Mike, shaken too, took a mirror out of the pocket of his tight pants and stared with undisguised contempt at the reflection of the cold, obdurate face, chin thrust out. He touched a few light lines on his forehead with self-disgust, then managed a smile to impress me. "I carry this mirror because I have to see what I look like before I hustle a new score. Red doesn't need to do that. He looks like a fag because he is and the scores can tell."

"I guess youth among gay hustlers is more important than among Vegas chorus ponies," I remark to Harold after telling him of Mike and Red.

"Sure," he answers. "The gay men who buy hustlers must persuade themselves they're getting something for their money; something that's not available for free. I've heard gay men use that phrase over and over again, telling themselves and each other they're paying for a little temporary contact with youth they wouldn't want permanently anyhow.

"The whole gay world's a big wheel of people kidding themselves, you see, for as long, God help us, as we're able."

But Harold is less interested in hustlers and their problems than in how a man like himself begins the search for companionship and—yes—sex, though unpaid for, in the labyrinthine homosexual hangout of a city he doesn't know.

Of course, there *is* the homosexual grapevine but it is
not nearly as extensive as men like J. Edgar Hoover and
Duane Barker say it is. Only a minority of gay people
have sufficient contact with their own to become exposed
to it. They are the only ones who know the gay streets
(not necessarily the hustling ones) where two gay stran-
gers can make contact in a strange town.

"But even if you know the streets," I ask, "how do you
make the contacts? Suppose a straight man's walking on
a gay street and you . . ."

Harold smiles. "That's a hazard, all right. But when
you're in sufficient need of something, you take chances.
You start out ambiguously to pick up a man who may
look interesting to you. What I do is to approach a
strange man in a way he can take or leave. For instance, I
might ask him if he had the time. If he told me pleas-
antly, I'd make some inane follow-up remark. I'd say, 'My,
I didn't realize it was still so early.' " Harold's clenched
hands belie his flipness.

"And then?"

"Well, hopefully, he'll speak now without further encouragement from me."

"What might he say?"

Harold laughs. "Oh, some brilliant thing like, 'Would
you by any chance have a cigarette on you?' I'd give him
a cigarette, light it for him."

When he was young and still believed in God, Harold
literally used to pray as he lit some pickup's cigarette:
"Let this work out. Make him really what he looks to be.

Don't have him be another one-night stand. I want to love him and have him love me in return."

After something like the cigarette incident, Harold says he would keep looking for ways of keeping the conversation alive and going. Still casually, although by now he would be seeking the suggestion of a clue—one a straight man wouldn't recognize but a gay man would, "I might talk about the weather. I'd say something like, 'It's a little cool tonight, isn't it?' And my pickup might answer, 'I don't know about that. I'm a little hot myself.' There's a double entendre there, you see, a clue . . ."

So Harold might afford himself the luxury of an even more pertinent comment. "You know, I hate Saturday nights (or whatever the particular night happens to be). For me, they're the loneliest nights in the week." Laughing, he might glance at his companion covertly, gauging the effect of his remark. Ready, always, to follow up with other words delivered in a different tone and calculated to produce a different mood.

"Saturday night's the loneliest one in the week for me, too." If the other man responds in such a way, Harold may grow bold and suggest a walk. Or if the companion has sufficiently revealed himself in voice and manner, he may dispense with subtlety and speak frankly.

"How about a couple of beers or something. I don't want to go to a fancy place or anything. Just a fun place with people laughing and letting their hair down. *Gay,* you know."

There. Finally, the word's out. And if the man says he

would like to go to a gay place, Harold *knows* he is a homosexual like himself.

They may stop in a gay place and have their beer. Or again, they may not. They may be obsessed with their physical need to the exclusion of all else. How exciting this meeting, with someone who was so recently a stranger but who *may* become close to you, the permanent companion you have longed for. It happens seldom, of course, "maybe once in a blue moon, to one person out of hundreds, thousands. But you can always hope."

After we have been to several elegant homosexual restaurants and bars, Harold takes me to some homo-bohemian places in the Tenderloin. Here are the queens in female clothes and the "hair-fairies" not only in drag but with long, teased hair or wigs.

The men in black leather jackets are here, too, not the cyclists but the sadists who adorn their jackets with a huge *S* and the others whose *M*s advertise their masochistic leanings. Generally, they congregate in their own bars and when they do walk the Tenderloin, they do it either out of indifference or a sense of exhibitionism, daring those who disapprove to pick fights with them.

Women, too, are part of this scene. Topless dancers and prostitutes and pornographic models who take the tricks that come their way, competing for the hustlers' scores.

Harold stops and introduces me to six young hustlers. Two of them, Gene Luv and Lee Lynch, I know of course—they played in Harvey Mann's pornographic movies. There are four others, and no matter how carefully you appraise them for outward signs, they seem ordinary kids—almost indistinguishable from each other: they have good, athletic builds, long and slim, heavy in the chest, and they wear their mod clothes well —like the middle-class heterosexual kids I know back home. One boy, however, does stand out: he is beautiful. He is slimmer, less strongly built than his companions, although he has the same long limbs. Whereas the other boys have fine tans, his skin is marble white. His curly hair is blue-black, his mouth curves up at the corners and his eyes are sea blue, brooding eyes. He is delicate, like Gene Luv. His name, Harold says, is James Barton. The other three Harold introduces merely by their first names, Justin, Lewis and David.

James Barton is nineteen but "often passes for seventeen; with scores, you know." His voice is very quiet.

"I tell him he could pass for sixteen if he wanted," Justin says. "I mean, he looks at least two years younger than I do. And I'm eighteen."

Lewis and David agree with Justin. All of them are completely serious in their discussion of James' youth. It is obvious, listening to them, that he is the reigning prince here on the Tenderloin. Indeed, all these boys are unusual, Harold tells me; except for Gene and Lee, they are college students, who, incredible as it may seem, are paying their tuition and other college expenses with their hustling proceeds.

"Not only that," says Harold, "they all mean to continue living and working on the Tenderloin when they graduate."

"Yes," David, a pre-law student at San Francisco State, says, "we're going to college and helping the kids who need us on the Tenderloin like we needed other kids to help us when we first came here."

Much of the credit for their intense dedication to the Tenderloin, they tell me, belongs to the ministers of the local Glide Memorial Church of San Francisco, a Methodist church, one of the most compassionate and humane institutions of its type, which has managed not only to welcome the most forsaken and rejected Tenderloin kids, but, as David says, "to make us feel what we haven't felt ever—part and parcel of the human race."

"The fabulous ministers they've got," James says. "There's a man there now, a black, who really *really* speaks the kids' language. When he's around where the prostitutes are, the police won't hurt them, where ordinarily they'd beat hell out of them. That squad that covers the Tenderloin—they're called, or anyway, used to be before Glide, 'the shit squad.' "

"Saturation squad," Harold corrects.

"The kids called them the shit squad because we knew that everyone in the neighborhood thought of us as shit," James states. "Like on Eddy Street. This police sergeant around Eddy is hell on the prostitutes. And this one night he's getting ready to give them the business, so Cecil, that's this black minister's name, walks in. And all of a sudden, the police sergeant acts like he doesn't

have a thing against the prostitutes on Eddy Street. He's
just there doing a protective job. He says, 'Hello, Reverend.'

"As Cecil says, 'I don't care what they call me, 'Black
Nigger' or anything else, I'm here to help the people,
God damn it; and if they don't want my help, then it's
their own damn fault.'

"That's just the way he talks." James laughs boisterously.

Glide Memorial Church has helped the Tenderloin
kids organize themselves into a self-aid, virtual pressure
group. And other agencies, social and legal service
agencies the ministers contacted in the kids' behalf (and
even the San Francisco Police Department, through its
community relations service), cooperate with the Tenderloin kids. They chose the name Vanguard for their
"pressure group." James is president and Justin vice-
president.

I ask James what he thinks Vanguard has accom-
plished.

"Well," he says, considering it, "the kids no longer
feel helpless in the face of what they've regarded as au-
thoritarian ruthlessness.

"We've come to know many straights through our
work and they've come to know us. There isn't that great
a separation between us any more. We try to see the
right and wrong of it, like when the straight businessmen are wrong in the way they treat our kids, like throwing the hair-fairies out of restaurants because they tease

their hair, we tell them then that this is a free country and people can still dress and do their hair any way they want.

"But we don't consider ourselves the kids' guardians either. I mean, our kids steal from the businessmen. There's no use saying they don't. Sometimes they've got reason. And sometimes they're just mad. Or they do it for the fun. You know, trying to prove we can put things over on the straight.

"Like me. I was always a hell of a good hustler. Then I peddled junk and I did real good at that. You know something, I didn't even need the junk money because the hustling was so great—I get a bang out of going with guys, especially rich ones who are willing to pay and pay high for my energy [the homosexual term for sexual intercourse]. But I peddled because a lot of the junkies were straights and I got a bang out of messing them up more than they were already.

"Anyhow, I have to laugh now when I find myself telling the Tenderloin kids what they ought to do; telling them to be right with other people because not all of them hate them like the straights they knew before they came to S.F. and discovered our church."

Harold, still brimming with pride over the young hustlers, takes me to another club, less elegant than the first one but "smart" all the same. Also small and favored by the young marrieds. Two handsome young men in tuxedos sing their college songs, interrupting the quiet orchestra playing popular dance tunes. No one is dancing.

There is a steep cover charge here too, but the liquor list is long and exotic, the drinks described in such ecstatic terms that you would like to try them all. And the food is superb and carefully served. The men seem manly and expensively but tastefully, though not conservatively, dressed. There are two women besides me, both call girls, Harold tells me, who for their mutual convenience have contracted marriages with homosexuals; the girls don't really like men and the homosexual husbands serve as their cover-ups—as do they for the homosexuals, whose jobs and professions require that they be married. The husband-wife teams like each other, feel a real loyalty toward each other; sexually, however, they go their own ways without resentment and, in fact, often laugh and talk over their individual conquests.

Here, too, there are few queens and no hair-fairies. The reason for this, as anyone who knows the homosexual community understands, is that there are few overtly effeminate men in the majority of upper-class gay circles. Most of these, even if they needed to, couldn't afford the luxury of being overt, wearing makeup or swishing or tweezing their brows. Even so, there are often some slight signs, at least to the trained observer: an inflection of the voice, a characteristic stance or walk, a way of holding a cigarette that outgraces a woman's gracefulness.

Many homosexuals do not find it necessary to go beyond these subtle disclosures—certainly not to the lengths of displaying an effeminacy which, because they are physical men, can never make them women but only female caricatures. "And who the hell, if he has any self-respect, wants to turn himself into a caricature? True homosexuals are attracted not to caricatures of women but to men, virile, masculine men," Harold says.

But what about the small minority of coy, pretty, even beguiling queens, the few who aren't female impersonators? "If homosexuals generally don't like them, who are *their* lovers?" I ask.

"Well," Harold says, "mostly straights. Old goats who can't perform normally or young men who think the queens are girls when they pick them up. With the young men, the queens perform homo style. Usually, if men they've picked up ask for ordinary relations, they say they're menstruating. The excuse may work and it may not. And most of queens' pickups are what they call rough trade. They'd as soon as not beat the daylights out of them. That's why so many get hurt, beaten. A great many do; a very great many."

The queens, of course, are often quite disturbed emotionally. One Harold knows is named Alietta Jones. She is tawny-skinned and her teased hair is dyed a bright red. "Lambie pie," she asks Harold in a childish whisper, "how do you like my new hair color? Dig: my hairdresser done it for free all the time he talked, talked, talked. I fell asleep when he was talking. And maybe he didn't even know it, or maybe he didn't give a fuck. Pretty shade though, hunh?"

Another teased-haired queen, dressed in bright colors and beaming at us sweetly, chirps merrily, "Hello, hello, hello." Turning to Harold, she says, "Savior, hello." Har-

old says she changes names with the "numerous life-
stories she's got on tap, telling different stories to different people. Her name, one time I remember—that was
when she'd met a rich daddy who thought she was r-e-a-l
and took her home to meet his mother—was Marie Geraldine Antoinette."

"Did his mother think she was r-e-a-l too?"

"She never said. The time I saw her after that,
though, her name was plainer, Mary Ruth or something
like that. And she'd met another daddy who thought she
was r-e-a-l. He flipped over her and she would have
flipped over him. Only he was too p-o-o-r and it would
never do when you were accustomed to wealth to try to
make it with a poor daddy."

Harold sighs over Marie Geraldine Antoinette or
Mary Ruth or "whoever she is tonight. You know, people are so cruel. I mean gays as well as straights. A gay
who's made it as we say—so he's respectable on the surface, who's educated or financially well-off—would be
as unlikely as any straight to help a poor mixed-up
queen like that. Or a mixed-up hustler, either. They'll
cultivate the proper ones but reject the others. I understand the reasons, of course; but it bothers me all the
same.

"Because they can be helped. I don't know too much
about the queens but I do the hustlers. You saw it yourself. Not all, of course, but enough to make it worth-
while *can* be helped if the rest of us who've forgotten
we're outside the pale ourselves would only make an

effort. All people see are their tough exteriors. That's their advantage in trade. But some have got something underneath." He smiles nervously. "They care and that's a lot more than some respectable people do."

XI

"Using the Mails to Send Pornography to Nuns Makes Me Mad!"

I was first introduced to the big business of mail-order underground pornography by John Reid, a lawyer, who after fifteen years resigned from the post office obscenity squad whose prime job it is to ferret out mail-order pornographers and, hopefully, put them out of business. The squad, as it operates today, is a controversial one. Some people say it engages in the most arbitrary and undemocratic moral muzzling. And others believe that it does not sufficiently protect the rights of innocent people.

John Reid, despite having resigned "because I couldn't stand the damn job anymore," expresses both points of view coherently and intelligently.

"Well, let me say that two or three things really bug me as a taxpayer, as well as a former departmental lawyer. To begin with, I'd like to see the inspection service (which includes the twenty-three-man postal obscenity squad) ride herd only on the obscenity which the demurring people dislike *and* which comes to them unsolicited through the U.S. mails. That's a big enough job in itself, so there's really no time to work with the fellows who distribute their stuff to those who want it. To hell with them, the gullible ones who believe the phony ads they get. If they order from the pornography ads and are exploited, that's their business, not the squad's.

"The people who are repelled or frightened or what have you by the pornographic come-ons, the ads coming in the mails for no reason they can figure, and who write and telephone the squad about it—*they ought to be protected*. But the squad ignores them and instead goes after the distributors who release their material in shops and other legitimate outlets where those who want pornography can get it.

"Some of the people who contact the post office department because of stuff they can't stomach . . . they're a surprising bunch, really. See, the mail-order boys have so little notion about the people they solicit, they've even contacted Congressmen and Senators. And priests, rabbis and ministers. Nuns, too, with the most obscene —certainly to them I imagine—ads in creation.

"The Congressmen"—John smiles and shrugs—"don't bother me. They take their advertisements and show them all over the place and yell their hypocritical heads off in the local newspapers their sanctimonious constituents are sure to read about 'what is this country coming to' and 'we are deteriorating morally in this day as Rome and Greece did in theirs.' You can bet they won't buy it though, the advertised hokum, I mean.

"I'm not a Catholic, you know, and I'm not even religious in the accepted sense, but, honestly, I get chills running down my spine at the thought of nuns receiving such advertisements as some of those pornographers send. Just them. They're the ones I feel terrible about."

One reason mail-order pornographers solicit people who couldn't possibly want their goods is that they are gambling, playing a game that may yield them thrilling profits if they win. And if they lose, they really don't forfeit much.

"They obtain their lists, buy them from all sorts of odd people and places," Reid says. "Mostly, of course, they get them from brokers. And they're *so impersonal*—brokers' lists, I mean. A broker may sell any list he gets his hands on, including some he begs, borrows or steals, or rather, gets other people to beg, borrow or steal for him. The nun clientele, I would assume, comes from the last category, the stolen list. I've known brokers who are considered praiseworthy members of their community and their church. They are active donors and 'father's helpers' who are held in high esteem and often elected to office, which gives them access to lists of church members (these may be obtained or made up from their acquaintances within the church by almost any member) but, more important, to correspondents, clerical and lay: priests, ministers and rabbis from other churches and synagogues. The same is true also of charitable organizations to which they and their employees belong.

"Brokers, of course, have many sources aside from church and charity for obtaining lists of prospective clients. Real estate firms sell or give away contracts' names. And there are also neighborhood associations, PTA's, professional groups, ranging all the way from the American Guild of Variety Artists to the American Medical Association. They'd never sell names, of course, but neither would they tend to mistrust members, especially working, assiduous, untiring members, who request to see membership lists.

"Some of the people who work for those porno-list brokers are cards," John says. "Others, of course, don't know because their brokers don't tell them; brokers each have their individual ways of working and soliciting workers. As I've said before, all they have in common is their money and canniness."

I interviewed some of the people who work for such brokers—people living in Detroit, Cleveland, Cincinnati—cities recommended to me by John. As he had predicted, some of the employees had films over their eyes, really did not know the uses to which the names they provided their bosses would be put. Others knew and admitted they did. And some knew, but pretended they didn't.

In Cleveland I met a Mrs. Bohack, a knobby housewife smelling of ammonia and furniture polish. She wore a long-outdated poppy-covered hat during our first meeting in a downtown restaurant, where she had obviously never been before.

"The way I get my names is that I got a husband and three sons belong to unions and lodges and two daughters belong to ladies' groups, auxiliaries. And my two daughters got husbands belong to labor unions too. So I get

my names from all of them and sell them to Mr. K
my boss in New York.

"And when I run out of old names, new joiners c
along. Sure, I don't earn much from my work, but w
you love your family and want them to have everyth
you never did like I want for my grandchildren to ha
—well, every little bit helps."

With a decent citizen's and devout churchgoer's r
spect for morality, Mrs. Bohack says her complacen
world was rocked when Mr. Kandel first contacted he
about soliciting names for his lists. He is one broker who
tells prospective employees the truth about the uses of
the lists they secure him.

Mr. Kandel, she says, had been led to her by a neighbor who told him about her and her menfolk's many contacts. Amidst the clamor of factory sirens, the distant
puff and rumble of the trains pulling in and huffing out
in the station not too far from the frame house, "Papa
and I live in all alone now that the kids gone off and got
married and left us by ourselves, Mr. Kandel made his
proposition to Papa and me. And all the kids were there,
too, with their wives and husbands. Right at first, I
didn't know what he was talking about. Then, when I
did, I told him 'no' right away.

"That man," she says, taking a large bite of cherry pie
à la mode, "don't quit with a person's first answer. He
just won't take no, you know. I mean, for hours and
hours he was driving me crazy with his nagging. And
when I still say, 'No, I won't keep a list for such as that,'
he stops nagging on me and begins on the boys and Papa.

" 'You like to read sexy books?' he asked them." She reddens. "Even, now, after all these years, I can't say the word 'sexy' without blushing.

"So like I say, when that Mr. Kandel sees I won't do what he wants, he starts on my kids, my boys. And them with their wives sitting there." She repeats, "He asks the boys, my sons and son-in-laws both, do they like to read sexy books. And I answer for them. 'My boys come from a nice family. My daughters' husbands come from a nice family too.' Believe me, I think the world about my daughters' husbands. I won't say I love them and go on about them like my own children. They're fine men, not the kind to do wrong things.

"Men," she adds, however, "especially the young ones, they think they're smart because they went to school and read a few books. But they don't know any-thing about life. Right in front of his wife, my daughter, this one son-in-law starts saying, yes; he likes to read 'sexy' books sometimes. Then all the boys say the same; my *own sons* do it. And this Mr. Kandel, he even gets Papa to say he likes to read dirty books sometimes."

She looks at me wonderingly. "Doctors say there's nothing wrong with men reading those sexy books. They say most men read them. Pa told me and then showed me it was true in some books some doctor wrote. Imagine!"

Mrs. Bohack says that knowing all that now, she doesn't feel *quite* so guilty as when she first began her job. Besides, "it's so good" to be able to indulge her grandchildren with the money she makes. Her children claim that she spoils the grandchildren, but she couldn't

care less about any of that talk. "That's what grandmas are for," says Mrs. Bohack, supplier of pornographic lists, "to spoil their grandkids."

Love of money is a social disease most people hide as shamefully as if it had been caught from a whore. Not Robert M. Kandel, though. To him the accumulation of dollars is a religion, and he is grateful for the Puritanical laws in this country which have turned him into a near millionaire. He and his wife, Beatrice, live in an elegant house in Long Island with a mammoth swimming pool and a driveway lined with weeping willows. Beatrice is long-legged and slender, with jet-black hair and cat-green eyes. She is also a good twenty years younger than her fifty-three-year-old husband, a Russian Jew with a slight accent, a lusty man with a compulsion to reveal (even before being asked) his business dealings.

"I get my lists from a lot of people nobody'd expect," he says. "Sure, take that Bohack—I got lots like her. But also I got clothing salesmen and showgirls and saloon-keepers and hotel managers and reporters on newspapers and magazines, especially weeklies and monthlies. And I got politicians and nurses and doctors and lawyers. I mean society doctors and lawyers; people would be surprised. Oh, and prostitutes that send me names of their customers. Some prostitutes they got customers coming back and back to them. Some got sick men can't get a woman without pay. And the sick ones—my competitors should only never find it out— they're the best customers in the world. Yeah, also I got

Army fellows, and clerks and bailiffs and policemen and the owners and managers of the lonely-hearts' clubs. And, you know, the over-forty clubs; they're fine for business too. Not only the men in those clubs; there's women there also like to read what my customers got to sell them.

"Marriage-brokers too. And this, it's harder to believe than anything else, I also got funeral directors working. Do *they* send me a *lot of names!* In my Irisher neighborhood where I grew up when I was a Jewish boy, they said: 'There is always enough money for a shroud.' So when a man's wife dies and he don't want to hurt her family's feelings by taking up with somebody else too soon, there is always enough money for what I got to sell them men. It keeps them happy, and it keeps the dead wife's relatives thinking the husband is a wonderful man. It's nice for everybody—no? Also I got marriage clerks supply me with names. And insurance agents."

Mr. Kandel pays, he says, anywhere from one hundred to two thousand dollars for the purchase of a thousand names depending on their potential as buyers of pornography. And he rents lists for six to one hundred dollars for a thousand names. Naturally, he never sends his list to the renting pornographer, never shows it to him; instead, the pornographer mails the ad material to his office, where he and his staff then send it out to the potential customer.

The lists he buys cheaply for one hundred dollars, say, are the least likely to contain names of legitimate pornography buyers. They usually have *verboten* names of people who might complain to the post office personnel and so get the pornographer-renters in trouble. Mr. Kandel expects to lose customers when he uses such lists. But the ones for which he pays two thousand dollars himself and in turn charges his rental customers one hundred dollars for a single rental are generally combed for legitimacy. "I could use *them* a lifetime," he says.

Robert Kandel is worried about what recent court rulings will do to his business. What will become of them now that "people'll be able to just walk in a store and buy books and pictures they want, anything. What's with those Supreme Court judges anyway? And how far do they think to go to make America (God forbid) a country where stores can sell everything people want till the brokers will be forced out of business. And to this America is coming." In the ghetto of his boyhood, they would call such a country, "America Moishe Kapoyer." "Moishe Kapoyer" is a Yiddish fictional character, a sort of lovable idiot who does everything backward or upside down—anyhow exactly the opposite of what the rational person would expect. "So if America, after all this time, lets people buy what they want in bookstores and see what they want in movies—it would be 'Moishe Kapoyer.' A whole country full with idiots. . . .

"And that Supreme Court—mmm, idiots among idiots, them judges. Any grown-up, he wants to read something so . . . fine. He wants to read . . . so fine, why not. Everything should be there in the store, right out on the counter.

"But, at least the children . . . they can still be customers of my business. Because the Supreme Court, thank God for little things, says the stores can't sell to children under seventeen no pictures showing ladies' busts with no clothes. They got to wear clothes. Also, the Court says storekeepers who sell anyone under seventeen books with sex, they can go to prison for that. . . .

He laughs slyly. "So that leaves for me the ones under seventeen . . . it's a small favor but better than nothing. Because a boy sixteen, fifteen, twelve maybe—he is going to write and say he is twenty-one, not his real age. And if I don't see him with my own four eyes, how am I suppose to know he is only a boy and not a man? So maybe I can stay in business yet with the young ones can't buy in the stores. That is my only hope . . . them young ones. For now it is my hope. But there's this Congressman from Wisconsin, Zablicki, Zablocki,* a smart man. Yeah, *he* is going to put me out of my business if he passes his law. The way that will be is like this . . . he says all us brokers got to register with the post office. And we got to answer any questions the post office says answer. The Postmaster General, any questions he got, I got to answer him and tell him the truth. So everybody knows he's going to say right away, 'Listen, Mr. Kandel, I want to know the names of all your customers.' And if I say no, I won't tell him, where do I go? The jail, that's where. So I got to tell him what he wants. Natural. And my customers, once they know I got to do

* He is referring to Congressman Clement J. Zablocki, Democrat from Wisconsin, who has introduced legislation still under consideration aimed at the powers behind mail-order pornographers, list brokers like Robert M. Kandel.

that, I don't blame them if they don't stay customers no more. I'd be the same way, too.

"So you know what they can do, the customers? They can throw me out altogether, and exchange their own lists. We don't need Kandel, that big-shot with all his lists, they can say. We get less names, but anyways we won't have to worry about him squealing and us getting picked up."

The distributors, especially the younger men and few women among them, already exchange lists with one another instead of renting or purchasing them from brokers like Mr. Kandel. As one young distributor with many friends in the business says, "You don't need to go to the brokers if you play your cards right and know enough people in the business. All you've got to do is to get yourself put on the lists and you'll see what'll follow. It's like belonging to a pyramid club. Just from two lists, say, you might get two hundred different kinds of ads. Try it and see."

I wrote two letters in my husband's name to companies the distributor suggested, and, as he had foretold, we received so many ads from different companies (in addition, of course, to those I had contacted) that I could hardly find space for them all. They laid at my husband's feet such vendibles as erotic books, magazines, records, still and moving pictures of Hollywood stars, not starlets—"well-known names you'd never suspect to do this," one ad read, "cavorting in the nude and engaging in all manner of inflammatory precoital and coital positions you don't know exist," manuals to teach him to become a "better, a superb lover, so no woman can resist you; everyone of the feminine gender within your orbit will come under your spell and beg for more of what you'll have to give after you read our book." They offered also various items of apparel "for your sweetheart or wife." They were really withering toward wives, spelling the word "wife" in small letters of humble print while lauding SWEETHEARTS (invariably pluralized) in elephantine displays of capital letters.

Here are but a few of my solicitations:

The Curiosities of the Sexual Appetite Explored
APHRODISIACS & LOVE STIMULANTS (With chapters on the Secrets of Venus). At last, the works of famous John Davenport have been put into one volume! A virtual mine of out-of-the-way information on: Love Potions, Love Philtres and Powders, Special Preparations and Recipes—all used to increase sexual vigor and potency. Discover why mandrake was used to increase virility. What was the strangely sadistic aphrodisiac employed by the Amazons? Is there any truth to the myth of cantharides or Spanish Fly? All the answers and more are given along with the author's (and others') erotic experience! Other sections of this remarkable book deal with Ancient Phallic Worship, Virginity and Chastity, Marriage, Circumcision, Eunuchism, Hermaphrodism, etc. It would be virtually impossible to find so much information on these and on other sexual subjects—especially from little-known and even forgotten sources—within the covers of any other single volume!

* * *

NUDES AROUND THE WORLD

Something different, something new, something hot and spicy! Girls from nearly every country in the world . . . appearing as luscious, unblushing nudes! Africa invites inspection, Asia delights in comparison, cool northern Europe vies with Latin southern Europe, tropical South American beauties show themselves to be as sultry as those from either Australia, North or Central America! All the continents, most of the countries of the world . . . represented by exciting, exotic, tempestuous NUDES!

*   *   *

"MIZU SHOBAI" by Boye DeMente

Bizarre Forms of Oriental Lust Revealed! Authentic Case Histories reveal Japanese men and women, pursuing all forms of sexual ecstasy with fanatic dedication! Miss Y . . . a seductive "kept woman" confesses: *"Once we begin to make love I am not conscious of any sex taboos . . ."* Find out about Japanese bosses and secretaries who have a noon sex-break where "they take great delight in touching or licking their naked bodies!" Read the words of the Japanese woman who, in intimate detail, describes her specialty of pleasing foreigners—the ravenous, insatiable Italians; the cruel, dominating Turks; the bizarre habits of the Greeks! Find out about abandoned Oriental sex rites practiced in Japanese "love-hotels"! Learn why one kind of woman is called O'name, meaning one who licks or is licked! Selections in this blazing exposé include: An International Sex Spree at the Tokyo Olympics: Teen-Age Pleasure Girls: Pleasure Girls and Playboys: How Hostesses "Stimulate" Customers: Sex in the Foreign Colony: The Modern Kept Woman: Techniques of Having and Holding a Mistress . . . and many, many more!

From the "Instant Geisha" to the Tokyo brothel, this book churns with sex deviations and contortions as only the Japanese know them!

* * *

BUTTOCKS FETISHISM—A. Kind

Filled with actual photographs of the female buttocks in the nude and wearing wispy undergarments. Many True Case Histories of male and female fetishists.

* * *

BREAST FETISHISM—C. Morseck

All sizes, shapes, ages and colors of seductive women bare their delectable breasts in this photographic study of the nude breast! Filled with true Case Histories.

* * *

GENTLEMEN PREFER BRONZE—A Collector's Item in as many ways as you can collect! Every shade, every hue of dusky loveliness is revealed in this torrid exposé of Bronze Beauty. They'll dazzle you . . . they'll stir your senses . . . they'll bring you on like it hasn't happened since!

* * *

PRIVATE/PERSONAL: These are for your Personal Use *Only,* and I trust you will do just that.

Youth and Beauty—and Joan, my youngest model, offers you both. Only 14 years, very inexperienced in modeling, but the way she wears her "see-through" panties and nylons will surprise, and if I may add, please any man. *A very revealing set.*

Only 14½ years, with the Eastern look, and very well-matured in all her curves—bust full and firm—thighs very well-developed—posing in her own exciting way in the *nude* and a few with just a small fancy bra and "see-through" panties just to make you look and admire the young figure covered just that little bit—very exciting, revealing set of photos of a lovely young girl. Contains 10 fabulous shots that are for men who like the young figure. A Must.

A Truly Rare Set—A fully matured woman of 48 years —Bust of 47 inches, very well-developed thighs—posed for you in fully revealing *nudes*. This rare set of photos were taken in Private for the Collector of good rarities. 10 Adult shots.

Pure Naked Beauty—10 sizzling *Full Nude* photos of some of the most daring, full-blooded girls and women I have posed. Full lengths and some close-ups, showing you these lovely girls as they really are—they almost reach out to you in these privately taken photos of females with a "lot" to offer—and DO. Very good camera angles used.

A 20-year-old Irish girl with the mostest—her bust is all of 47 inches—photographed in *Full Nude* positions that will be sure to please. She's daring and most revealing in *All* her photos. Her fully matured charms give you all the details and the positions increase your pleasure. Her soft skin and lovely well-developed thighs will more than please you. Lovely long legs and mostly her very daring way offers you what you want in these *Fully Naked Photos.* Private sitting.

Full Frank *NUDES*—A mixed set of photos of some of my most lush girls and women (ages from 14 to 35). All of these photos were taken in *private* sittings and show these lovely girls revealing their *fully naked* figures to the *utmost,* in all positions that you seek. These females all have very well-built figures, good solid thighs and upright busts (39 inches to 48 inches). You will find these are exciting photos taken for *Adult Men*. They will delight and surprise you. They offer you photos taken in a very relaxed way giving you much pleasure in looking and looking again and again. Full set of 20.

Fabulous full *NAKED* Photos—Of a beautiful English woman; this lady has the fully matured figure that will delight. Bust 48 inches, very firm and upright, solid hips of 40 inches and really lovely thighs, very rounded. These nudes are photographed in strict *private* for the *private collector*. She reveals herself in *all* her glory in the *most relaxed* way. She's very well-matured in *all* her *ways*. You will see how she delights. Very good-looking.

There are numerous other offers of nude stills of women. And although I have never placed an order or written another letter after the first two, they keep coming and coming.

Mr. Kandel is grudging toward the pornographers, since recent court rulings will deprive them of a substantial number of their adult customers.

"But it hurts me, too, because I been living so good so long off the ones that bought my lists before the Court got such big hearts all of a sudden and says every grown-up should see what he wants, read what he wants. The judges in the Supreme Court should only drop dead. On account of them I got to lose everything; my house, my swimming pool, my car, my servants."

XII

A Skirmish in the Jungle:
"The Most Hated Guy in Town"

IT IS easy to see why nuns and the average man or woman, particularly those concerned that they may fall into the hands of their children, are bitterly opposed to such unsolicited mail-order advertisements. Yet even those who would reject such material for themselves and their families might believe that those who want it are entitled to it; by their very nature pornographers' ferreting campaigns must, as John Reid well knows, also reach those who want nothing to do with them. Banning pornography overtly allows it to exist covertly in the activities of the Robert M. Kandels. That, at least, was the case until May of 1967 when the United States Supreme Court cut through the veil of pretense and legalized girlie magazines and sexually erotic books of a type formerly held illegal in a decision that has come to be known as the Redrup ruling. It held, further, that adults who wanted overt erotica could seek it out in legitimate outlets rather than ordering it blind.

Though he did not specify it by name it was the

Redrup decision that caused "poor Mr. Kandel" to describe himself as becoming impoverished, and to attack not only the Supreme Court but the lawyers—strong civil libertarians who have been working for most of their professional lives for the freedom to read and to publish—lawyers like Robert Redrup for whom the Redrup decision is named, Ephraim London of New York and the famous California civil libertarian, Stanley Fleischman of Los Angeles.

I first met Stanley Fleischman after he had returned from Houston, Texas, where he had defended a client on seven counts of alleged obscenity, the publication and distribution of "poor men's pornographic books" called *Sin Summer, Swap Sect, Passion Carousel, Orgy Club, Shame Hunger, Temple of Shame* and *Virgins Incorporated.* He had been in Houston two months, "two long months; you could call them if you wanted to, my long, hot summer." No matter where he was during those months in Houston, walking down the street, sitting in a restaurant, having a sorely needed drink in the bar of his hotel after a hard day in the courtroom, he says he was conscious, always, of a warning shiver of trouble, of danger lurking everywhere for the "lawyer from L.A. who'd come to foist his dirty books on Houston. I guess there were those there who'd have lynched me if they could have. I'm not joking when I say I was the most unpopular guy in town. Unpopular, hell. The most hated guy in town."

Stanley Fleischman had mustered an imposing array

of witnesses for this landmark trial. Chief among them was the prominent New York marriage counselor Wardell B. Pomeroy. Dr. Pomeroy, in addition to practicing his present profession, is co-author with Alfred Kinsey of all his works including *Sex Behavior of the Human Male, Sex Behavior of the Human Female, Pregnancy, Birth and Abortion* and *The Sexual Offender.* He is also president of the Society for the Scientific Study of Sex and treasurer of the American Association of Marriage Counselors. The conclusion of the Houston trial is an illuminating example of the continuing battle fought by civil libertarians all over the country.

Fleischman began by asking Dr. Pomeroy whether in his investigations to prepare *The Sexual Offender* he found that persons convicted of sex offenses would be more sexually aroused from reading stories of a sexual nature than those who had not been convicted of such offenses.

The research team headed by Dr. Pomeroy and for which he conducted two-thirds of the interviews revealed "that the persons who were sex offenders, who had been arrested and convicted for sex offenses, appeared to be much *less* sexually aroused by reading stories . . . by pictures of a sexual nature, than those who were never arrested and convicted on any charge."

"Is there anything pathological or antisocial in owning books that cause sexual arousal or interest?" Fleischman asked him.

"No."

"Would you explain why you give that answer?"

"Well, because the act is so all-encompassing. You would have to call essentially the entire population pathological under these circumstances and the word loses its meaning when you do that."

Dr. Pomeroy said that among average men, not sexual criminals, "reading or talking about sexual matters is omnipresent, all about us in our culture—people being interested in sexual stimuli of any sort."

"Now, Doctor," Mr. Fleischman asked, "have you observed—well, you were with Kinsey in the Institute—in the last twenty years have you observed any change with regard to sexual candor? That is to say, in terms of the freedom with which sexual matters are handled throughout our society?"

"Yes. There has been a considerable change, certainly in the last twenty-five years. This has shown itself in many different ways. Certainly the freedom with which people talk about sexual matters is much more open now than it was during the thirties and the early forties. There are many more magazines, books, movies which have changed.

". . . In 1938, when the Institute first began, people were rather shocked that we would study such a thing as human sexual behavior. As time has gone on, there has been more and more freedom to make such studies. The Masters and Johnson book on *Human Sexual Response* contains research where people are actually observed having sexual relations."

Fleischman asked whether words, "previously taboo words, so-called vulgar words, the short four-letter words, are now being used openly and frankly, in specific books to which you have reference?"

Dr. Pomeroy said that the short four-letter words were "used openly and frankly in such works as *Lady Chatterley's Lover, Tropic of Cancer, Tropic of Capricorn, Sexus, City of Night, Candy.*"

"What about the word 'cunt.' Is that a word found frequently in current literature?"

Dr. Pomeroy calmly said that it was.

Fleischman asked whether or not a variety of sexual acts were described in the books of which Dr. Pomeroy was speaking, and Dr. Pomeroy said they were. Such acts are described in numerous other books also and he brought two: *The Story of O* by Pauline Reage and *The Writings of the Marquis de Sade.* Fleischman requested that he illustrate the variety of sexual acts he had reference to, and Dr. Pomeroy read aloud the following example of sado-masochism from *The Story of O*:

> . . . At the same time she heard a whistling noise in the darkness, O felt a terrible burning across her back. She screamed. Pierre flogged her with all his might. He did not wait for the screams to subside, but after he had struck, she went on screaming and tears streamed down on her open blouse. "Please be good enough to turn around," he said. Slipping the riding crop handle which pressed against her wrist when she was facing him, he moved back slightly and lowered his crop in front of her thighs as hard as he could. The whole thing had lasted five minutes.

Dr. Pomeroy read four other passages from *The Story of O* which similarly illustrate O's and her lover's sado-masochistic relations. He went on to read as "another illustration of one of the numerous varieties of sexual acts covered in present-day books," a passage from *The Writings of the Marquis de Sade,* who is explaining to his mistress, Eugénie, the acts in which he wishes to engage simultaneously with both her and a young virgin:

> The best way to go about it is for the woman to lie prone, contrariwise to her fucker and upon the man's body. He pops his prick into her mouth, his head being lodged between her thighs. He repays in kind what she does for him by introducing his tongue into her cunt, or by playing it over her clitoris. When employing this attitude, one must show spirit, catch hold of the buttocks and the partners should finger and tickle each other's assholes, a measure always necessary to complete voluptuous experience.

Dr. Pomeroy told the court that *The Story of O* had been published in hard cover and reviewed, favorably, in many newspapers, including the New York *Times.* As for *The Writings of the Marquis de Sade,* it had been published in both hard and soft cover and favorably, often very favorably, reviewed.

The passages he read aloud, he said, "are not at all unusual in these books. There are many such activities described."

Fleischman then asked Dr. Pomeroy whether the seven books on trial "*could* (not *do* but *could*) go beyond the customary limits of candor and descriptions and representations of matters pertaining to sex, nudity or excretion in the United States as a whole."

Dr. Pomeroy said that no, they couldn't, and Mr. Fleischman asked him to tell, very briefly, what the books are about.

Sin Summer, Dr. Pomeroy said, is the story of a young grocer's delivery boy, who, though basically interested in the girl next door, "has many affairs with many different women. He finally has intercourse with the girl and seduces her mother. He then joins the Army while his girl's mother goes to a psychiatrist who also seduces her."

Dr. Pomeroy said he believes there is "social significance" in the book and described it as "some talk about the tormenting sexual arousal, without fulfillment, of the girl's mother, and how she tried to cope with her problem. There is also talk about the corrosive relation between parents and children when they don't understand each other, or don't try to, and there is an exploration of the corrosion existing between husband and wife, the young girl's parents."

Dr. Pomeroy stated he believes that the ideas and concepts developed in *Sin Summer* are "definitely over and above the specific sexual experiences that happen here —over and above the entertainment value for which some people read it." He also believes that it would not appeal to the "prurient, the morbid or shameful interest of the average adult." On the other hand, the book "would arouse some people, not a great many . . . But certainly, there are some people whom it would arouse sexually. However, as far as depicting material that is bizarre, that is so out of the ordinary that people would develop a 'morbid and shameful interest' in it, I question that very much. I don't believe it would."

Mr. Fleischman then asked Dr. Pomeroy to outline *Swap Sect* which is a story about wife-swapping.

He said that one of the wives finds difficulty in obtaining orgasm with her husband, and they begin a system of wife-swapping which satisfies both for a while. "When, however, they tire of the sect or group with which they're affiliated, they find themselves unable to leave it because they are being blackmailed by someone who has taken motion pictures of both of them in compromising positions. Finally, the husband retrieves the pictures and he and his wife free themselves from the group."

He said that, like *Sin Summer, Swap Sect* does not go beyond the customary limits of today's candor.

"Now," Mr. Fleischman asked, "let's talk first about the kind of sexual description in the book. Is there any unusual kind of sexual descriptions that are not found in literature generally?"

"No, there are descriptions of intercourse, some rather euphemistic indications of mouth-genital contact. There is some female homosexuality in the book, but these are the sort of things that one reads in literature." And he believes, besides, that there are also in the book some matters of worth to the kinds of people who would buy and read it.

"It tells about the use of sex as a weapon, as a way of getting back at people. There is some information about the fact that forbidden sex, such as extramarital intercourse, may be more arousing to some people, just because it *is* forbidden, than marital intercourse.

"There is some talk about communication in marriage and the difficulty that husband and wife have when they can't communicate." When the husband and wife finally are able to communicate with each other, they eventually end up reconciled.

The third book, *Passion Carousel,* is the story of Libby, a banker's daughter who runs away from home and falls into the clutches of a rich sadist, Mal. It contains a series of sadistic scenes, involving a group of sadists and masochists who engage in a Black Mass, as they call it, an antireligious episode where they try to go as far as they can in terms of whipping and beating. Eventually, they murder two people in this Black Mass.

The book tells also of Libby's struggle to get out of this situation, her inability to cope with that life or to find some way out. She does finally meet a man who is ensnared by Mal's wife, and the two of them eventually do go to the police and confess their participation in these masochistic rites and presumably make some sort of adjustment with each other.

Dr. Pomeroy told the court that, according to his and his associates' researches, "there is a great interest— an undercurrent of sado-masochistic interest in people . . . in reading and fantasying about it."

Dr. Pomeroy found that *Passion Carousel,* as he did

the three preceding and would the three books to follow, met the Supreme Court definitions entitling it and
the others to First Amendment protection. And he
pointed out there is "certain good in the book, *again
for the kinds of people who are reading it . . . who
aren't, perhaps, as well-educated as many of us . . .*"

"Now," Mr. Fleischman asked, "in your practice as
a marriage counselor, have you found there is any value
in people's talking about sexual matters?"

"Yes, sir. Very often the very talking about sex helps
inhibited persons become less so, become more relaxed,
more willing to face their problems in regard to sex."

"Do you think reading about sexual matters has some
of the same value?"

"Yes, I have seen this in many instances."

He said that he believes the books on trial "may have
the same effect on the people, those for whom they're
written, as *Lady Chatterley's Lover* or *The Story of O*
has for their audience. They would arouse them sexually."

"Is there anything wrong with being aroused sexually?"

"Indeed not."

"Now, Doctor, taking the seven books, all the sexual
descriptions and recitations found in them, is there anything in them that has not been true to life in the sense
that some people, under some circumstances, have engaged in the conduct or have been caught up in any
events of like kind?"

"I could duplicate many of these scenes by people who have responded in our histories."

Fleischman's questions were concluded. He turned over the questioning to his associates, suaveloquent Percy Foreman of Candy Mossler trial fame, and Norman Schwartz. Foreman went directly to the question which so concerned Fleischman, asking it in his characteristic fashion:

"Dr. Pomeroy, as one who is—one who has dedicated his life to research in the field about which you have testified, don't you agree that the printed page is much too good for the common people?"

"No, I don't think I would agree to that."

"You do not hold to the theory that only the educated, the erudite, the economically blessed should have access to reading matter?"

"No, I don't."

"Is there a good purpose in making available reading matter to the people, perhaps with an eighth-grade education?"

"I think there is value in this."

Dr. Pomeroy said that he believes that the more discussion, the more open forums, the more books written on *any level*—"that of the Ph.D. or sixth-grade school dropout, must be valuable, not alone to sexual misfits but to all of us."

Norman Schwartz put into high relief what was brought out earlier, much earlier, in the trial and could bear repetition again—two full months later.

"Could you say, Dr. Pomeroy, whether or not these books we've been talking about—these seven books—provide a means of living vicariously, a means of escape entertainment to their readers?"

"They do."

"Would you say entertainment and escape values are important?"

"Yes."

Then it was Charles Sussman's turn. He spoke for the district attorney.

"Isn't it a fact, Doctor, that these books, any or all of them, or any part of them, would in fact have a quite detrimental effect on a person who had a psychological problem with regard to sex?"

Dr. Pomeroy believed the "books might be helpful . . . not universally deleterious at all."

"I was asking about people who had sexual problems."

"Yes, yes indeed. I was *talking* about such people."

"Tell me, Doctor," Mr. Sussman asked, "what is your definition of hard-core pornography?"

"My definition—and it is not the legal one—is that hard-core pornography is material deliberately conceived for the one purpose of producing strong sexual arousal, not titillation, but strong arousal. Also, it usually achieves its goal."

Dr. Pomeroy realized that Mr. Sussman's questions were calculated to influence the jury "to believe me," as Pomeroy put it, "far out on the whole subject of sex." At least four times, he asked what "the 'average person

—not you, Doctor, but the average person' would consider morbid and shameful in matters of sex."

The fourth time, Dr. Pomeroy "holding onto my cool though it wasn't easy" replied as though Mr. Sussman had asked a novel question. ". . . As you can imagine, I have pondered this concept for a long time, and am still, today, finding it difficult to resolve. There are some things that are bizarre, so unusual, so far away from the ordinary person's knowledge, they might be thought morbid and shameful. But I find it difficult to imagine what these might be."

Sussman asked for some examples.

"Well, extreme cases of people eating feces or excrement might fall into this category of morbid or shameful. But I think the average person is, as I have said, so interested in sex that though he would find this bizarre, he probably would not find it morbid and shameful.

"And, of course, there are some people in the world whose pattern of sexuality does embrace the eating of excrement or feces.

"Now, certainly, I am not referring to the average person. I am saying, though, that although the average person wouldn't eat feces himself, he might still be interested in people who do. If he read of such an incident in a book, for instance, he would not necessarily put it away or throw it away."

"Can you give us any other situation which would appear morbid and shameful to the average person—not to *you*, Doctor, to the *average person*."

"I did not say," Dr. Pomeroy answered, "that the situation I cited might necessarily appeal to the average person's 'morbid and shameful interest.' I said it would appeal to his bizarre interest.

". . . Well, I suppose the idea of people hanging from a chandelier would be bizarre since it is so different and unusual and might even shock some but I still would have difficulty in thinking of this sort of sexuality as appealing to average people's morbid or shameful interest."

"That would be amusing, wouldn't it?" Mr. Sussman asked. "Having intercourse that way . . . Well, what else besides hanging from a chandelier would be morbid or shameful?"

Dr. Pomeroy told Mr. Sussman—again—that there is a difference in the meaning of "bizarre" which is unusual and "morbid and shameful." "The average person might find the idea of intercourse while hanging from a chandelier 'unusual, different' . . . but not 'morbid or shameful.' These two are *very different words,* Mr. Sussman."

"We are just trying to get—you have given us your opinion that these seven books on trial here do not go beyond contemporary community standards."

"That's right."

"And that they do not appeal to the prurient interest and that they do have a value and all that. We would just like to see what the basis for these opinions are, Doctor. What would be bizarre in *your* opinion, *if anything?*"

"Well, as I said, like the average person I can conceive of coprophagia—eating feces—as being something that might be quite bizarre. But I've already told you that. I also think that necrophilia—this is having intercourse with a corpse—might be bizarre."

"But you're not even sure whether it would be?"

"Not one hundred percent."

Mr. Sussman returned to one of the questionable books, *Passion Carousel*. He talked of the most piquant part—the inflammatory antireligious Black Mass ritual and its attendant incidents. He said he would like to cite first "that passage where a girl is severely beaten and in a state of unconsciousness and the men use her for sexual relations. And then she subsequently dies. Would you characterize that as a morbid and shameful portrayal of sex?"

"This," Dr. Pomeroy said, "would certainly come close—yes." But he reminded Mr. Sussman of the Supreme Court ruling that "a work must be considered as a whole before it can be called obscene; a judgment of obscenity may not be made of a passage taken out of context."

Mr. Sussman cited other portrayals in the book that Dr. Pomeroy admitted would be "close to what is morbid and shameful" if taken out of context.

"And now," Mr. Sussman said, "what about the woman who had to perform oral copulation on every man in the group. Is this shameful and morbid? Would it arouse erotic interest?"

"I think there are certainly some American males who would be aroused by this material. But more would be merely titillated erotically—not aroused in the hard-core sense."

"What about the lesbian activities portrayed in the book?"

"Interestingly enough," Dr. Pomeroy said, "lesbian activities are of tremendous interest to the average American male, and I think one of the reasons is that if men, average men, are aroused by one female, then two females seem twice as good. They are not thinking of lesbianism as homosexuality; they are projecting their own male sexuality into the situation and it transforms into heterosexuality to them. This is my analysis as to why the male is interested in lesbian activities."

Mr. Sussman, turning now to the book on wife-swapping, asked whether it was medically possible that a woman's frigidity problems might be aided by swapping. Dr. Pomeroy said it was possible.

And so the trial went—question after repetitive question—as it had for months. However, because of Fleischman's main expert witness, his own technique and, importantly, the fact that changes are going on throughout the country, the jury was hung. Even Fleischman was surprised at this; knowing Houston as one of the most hidebound cities in the country, he had expected total defeat.

"Well, based on my case in Houston," Fleischman said minutes before he and Robert Redrup were to appear before the Supreme Court to argue the historic cases whose verdicts comprised the text of the Redrup decision, "I know we're going to win a great victory today. Not alone the people's freedom to read any books they want, but poor men's freedom to read *Love Lust* or *Swap Sect* as well as rich men's freedom to read *Marquis de Sade* or *The Story of O.*

". . . A wife-swapper or a blue customer . . . some derelict who masturbates in a Tenderloin movie while watching a naked girl playing volleyball and then goes out a little readier to face his dreary environment— what kind of culture do we live in to condemn that poor bastard for trying to make life a bit more bearable? Hell, he's not doing anything that doesn't come naturally to any man. Walking down the street, seeing a good-looking girl, a man's going to undress her in his mind.

"But forget about the derelicts. What about the people who are economically, even culturally of a class we hard-working, red-blooded Americans approve—the guys who have the right job and live in the right house and have gone to the right colleges? Only they like boys instead of girls? Well, figure the problem from two angles, i.e., first, why should their love life cause the rest of us to blow our stack? I mean what business of ours is it whom a man wants to go to bed with?"

Our inherent Puritanism has turned us into such fools really that we don't realize how comically far our laws go. "Take as an example the antisodomy laws [one example of the Puritanism Fleischman speaks of: America's laws against sodomy are surpassed only by those against kidnapping, murder and rape], laws aimed at heterosexual as well as homosexual couples. In Georgia the penalty for first-time sodomy ranges from one to ten years. A second conviction draws from ten to thirty years. In Massachusetts, a first-time sodomist receives a straight twenty years as he also does in Minnesota and Nebraska. Connecticut specifies a thirty-year sentence. In North Carolina a sodomist may receive from five to sixty years and in ultraliberal Nevada from one year to life. Forty-eight states specify that cunnilingus [oral contact by a man with the female genitalia] and fellatio [oral contact by a female with the male genitalia] are as serious an offense when performed by heterosexuals as by homosexuals.

"Well, you talk about sodomy among married couples, and, you know, you're approaching awfully close to home base for many of us. For it's not just the minority —homosexuals, say—but all of us, heterosexuals, married and unmarried, who can be punished for refusing to fit into the single-design for 'head-to-head lovemaking.' And here, when you consider the 'crimes' of fornication and adultery, you approach even closer. The little fact of 'universality' doesn't stop Connecticut, Dakota and Vermont from threatening adulterers with five-year jail sentences.

"The adultery laws are incomprehensible? Well, then, think of Indiana where heavy petting between boys and girls under twenty-one is considered criminal. We 'normal' people are just lucky that the lawmakers' evidence against us is so tough to get. Otherwise, so help me, there wouldn't be enough jails in America to hold us all!"

Fleischman is beginning to get help from unexpected

sources, some of whom once espoused the correctness of Puritan morality. Enlightened leaders of all denominations in the modern churches no longer inculcate their followers with guilt and fear over sex; some of them are among the most ardent upholders of a new morality, one in keeping with modern man's understanding of himself and his world.

The Reverend Dr. Joseph Fletcher of the Episcopal Theological School states in his *Twentieth Century Philosophy of Sex,* "The Christian churches must shoulder much of the blame for the confusion, ignorance, and guilt which surround sex in Western culture . . . The Christian church, from its earliest primitive beginnings, has been swayed by many Puritanical people, both Catholic and Protestant, who have viewed sex as inherently evil." The Reverend Dr. William Graham Cole, head of the department of religion at Williams College, accepting in no uncertain terms the sexual ideology of Kinsey rather than the Bible, writes in *The Bible and the World of Dr. Kinsey:* "There can be no quarrel with the secular world at this point. It is right and the Church has been wrong. Sex is natural and good . . . those who take the Bible seriously must stop apologizing for sex . . . they must begin with a concession to the secular mind, granting that sex is natural . . ." And Robert Shinn of the Union Theological Seminary does not hesitate to explain clearly and without apology why many Protestants "no longer wish to be identified with repression and Puritanism. . . . In recent years," he says, "Protestant theologians have reexamined these [Puritan] concepts. They now argue that Puritanism when it insists that sex is evil is actually a distortion of Christian doctrine . . ."

Stanley Fleischman, as he emphasizes time and again, fought only a "small skirmish" in Houston. But it is symptomatic of the great battle being waged all over America against the Puritan ethic which, once having created the world of underground sex in America, nourishes it, making the jungle flourish and grow thicker. Paradoxically, blows such as those struck by Stanley Fleischman, far from undercutting the good citizens of Houston, actually work to their benefit. Those who are really threatened are the Earl Jacksons, Harvey Manns, Jean Morgans, Robert Kandels—parasites who depend upon our hypocrisy to survive and thrive.

The Houston victory is now but a straw in the wind. But honest examination of one facet of America's Puritan Jungle inevitably must lead to honest examination of them all. And when that happens, those tragic souls now condemned to skulk in the underground will at long last be free. When that happens, such tragic victims of our hypocrisy as the Tenderloin kids, Gene Luv, Lee Lynch, Joanie and Bill, Anise; the sad exploited beauty queens, Ervie and even Rowena; the proud and secret swingers, Anita, Marlena, Joanne; the overt and covert homosexual leaders and hustlers, from Harold Call to James Barton, can at last come out into the open and live with the dignity and self-respect that are their due.